EX LIBRIS

SHEILA & JOHN MULLOY

EALAÍ ÉIREANNACH DEN tSEANRÉ CHRÍOSTAÍ

Françoise Henry

(Máire Nic Dhiarmada a d'aistrigh)

Arna chur amach do
Chomhar Cultúra Éireann
ag Cló Mercier
4 Sráid an Droichid, Corcaigh

EARLY CHRISTIAN IRISH ART

Françoise Henry

(Translated by Máire MacDermott)

Published for
The Cultural Relations
Committee of Ireland
by The Mercier Press
4 Bridge Street, Cork

© The Government of Ireland 1979

First Edition 1954

Second Edition 1962

Third Edition 1979

ISBN 0 85342 462 4

The aim of this series is to give a broad, informed survey of Irish life and culture, past and present. Each writer is left free to deal with his subject in his own way, and the views expressed are not necessarily those of the Committee. The general editor of the series is Caoimhín Ó Danachair.

Françoise Henry, after being on the staff of the Musée des Antiquités nationales, St Germain-en-Laye, belonged for a long time to University College, Dublin, where she was Director of Studies in Archaeology and History of Painting and then Head of the Department of History of Painting, until her retirement in 1974.

She has published many studies in Irish art, both in French and in English, the titles of which are given in the bibliography at the end of this booklet.

Design Jan De Fouw

Printed by Cahill Printers Limited, Dublin

TABLE OF CONTENTS

TEXT ILLUSTRATIONS

PLATES

1. Detail from bronze trumpet found near Armagh. (N.M.D.) *Phot. N.M.D.*
2. The " Petrie crown " (N.M.D.) *Phot. N.M.D.* (about 1/1)
3. *a* Openwork bronze disc from the River Bann (Ulster Museum) *from J.R.S.A.I.* (2/1)
   b Detail of enamelled penannular brooch (N.M.D.) *Phot. F. Henry* (2/1)
4. Enamelled bronze latchet (N.M.D.) *Phot.N.M.D.* (about 2/1)
5. Penannular brooch found in Ireland (Liverpool Museum) *Phot. F. Henry* (about 1/1)
6. *a* Enamelled bronze disc found in Lagore (N.M.D.) *Phot. N.M.D.* (1/1)
   b Enamelled bronze handle of hanging-bowl found in Winchester (B.M.) *Phot. B.M.* (1/1)
7. *a, c* Initials from the " Cathach " (R.I.A.) *Phot. F. Henry, G.S.*
   b Bronze brooch from Ardakillin crannog (Roscommon) (N.M.D.) *Phot. N.M.D.*
8. *a* Initial from the " Cathach " (R.I.A.) *Phot. F. Henry*
   b Book of Durrow, beginning of St. Luke's Gospel (T.C.D.) *Phot. G.S.*
9. Manuscript from the Library of Bobbio monastery (Ambrosian Library, D. 23 sup.) *Phot. F. Henry*
10. Engraved pillar, Reask (Kerry) *Phot. F. Henry*

I have pleasure in thanking here the Directors and Keepers of the Museums of Dublin, Belfast, Cork, Liverpool, Bergen, Stockholm and St. Germain-en-Laye, the Trustees of the British Museum and the British Library, the Dean and Chapter of Lichfield Cathedral, the Prefect of the Ambrosian Library, the Librarians of the Royal Irish Academy Library, Trinity College Library (Dublin), the Cathedral Library, St. Gall and the Bodleian Library, the Victoria and Albert Museum Photographic Service, the Royal Society of Antiquaries of Ireland, Methuen and Co., Publishers, Mr. J. Kennedy, of the Green Studio and the Editions Mélie, at Chauny (Aisne) for permitting me to photograph objects and manuscripts in their custody or for authorising reproduction of photographs or blocks belonging to them. And I want to express my gratitude to Miss Hilary Richardson, of the Department of Archaeology, University College, Dublin, whose vigilant and indefatigable exertions have made it possible to bring out this new edition. Apologies are due also to the translator whose original text of 1954 has been marred in successive revisions by additions and alterations.

Dublin, April 1978

EARLY CHRISTIAN IRISH ART

INTRODUCTION

PERHAPS NO ART has given rise to such contradictory statements, such violent enthusiasm and condemnations, as that which developed far from the storms which swept the Continent, in the Ireland of the early Middle Ages. Scholars of varied origins and training have paused, fascinated or irritated before its disconcerting enigma, for which they have advanced the most contradictory solutions. For Arthur Kingsley Porter it represents " a fundamental step in the the history of Western civilization, uniting the East with the West, dying Antiquity with the nascent Middle Ages. " Henri Focillon, who also looks to it for the sources of Romanesque art, eloquently describes it as " one of the most astonishing of human reveries, one of the most mysterious caprices of the intellect. " More recently, Mr. Masai, a Belgian scholar, states, " if Irish illuminations can inform us on the Irish people, it will certainly not be to teach us their high degree of civilization nor their good taste but rather to reveal to us a profound barbarism, trying to imitate as well as possible, more civilised neighbours ". And the learned Dom Henri Leclercq, usually of sounder judgement, has spoken of the " hateful caricatures of the Irish manuscripts ".

These remarkable differences of opinion should put us on our guard. Irish art must be approached with prudence. Its sphere is but vaguely defined in many minds and the interpretation of its historical and aesthetic import has led to the most conflicting pronouncements. Thus, without wishing to enter into details of the controversies, a procedure which would require weighty scientific equipment, it is nevertheless essential to indicate a few fixed points which definitely identify this art with Ireland and help to define it, while at the same time they suggest its position in the evolution of medieval art.

The difficulty which we experience when we attempt to define its character is due partly to the very antiquity of this art which reached

13

its zenith in the seventh and eighth centuries of our era, a time when documents clearly establishing the origin and date of a monument or object are rare. Another difficulty arises from the fact that of all the works of Irish artists it is the illuminations that enjoy the greatest fame. For nothing is more vagabond than a manuscript, nothing more difficult to tie to a precise origin; illuminated volumes travel from monastery to monastery, they are lent, they are sent to distant friends, they are copied and are carried about in the satchels of pilgrims or refugees. Their colophons* also may be falsified in the desire to attribute a manuscript to some celebrated saint. In consequence, nothing is easier or more tempting than to advance daring hypotheses concerning them and such indeed are not lacking. Recent publications attributing almost the whole mass of Irish illuminations to the monasteries of the north of England are a striking example of this kind of theorising.

The astonishing vigour of the expansion of the Irish church makes the problem still more complex. At the end of the sixth century, St. Columba left Ireland, to found on the west coast of Scotland the monastery of Iona, which, continually inhabited by Irish monks, remained for centuries an important focus of Irish culture. In the seventh and eighth centuries, Irish missionaries travelled throughout Scotland, England and the whole of Western Europe, founding monasteries to which they brought their art, and which remained for a long time in the closest possible contact with Ireland. One may mention examples such as Lindisfarne in Northumbria, Péronne in northern France, called for centuries " Péronne of the Irish ", and the foundations of St. Columbanus and his companions—Luxeuil in Gaul, St. Gall in Switzerland and Bobbio in Italy. Thus, many manuscripts may have been illuminated far away from Ireland by Irishmen, or, to complicate the problem further, by the pupils of Irish monks.

It is too often forgotten, however, that the illuminations belong to a series of works in the same style, some in metal, others carved in stone. Until recent years objects of metalwork seemed as difficult to place with certainty, as were the manuscripts. The exhibition cases of the Museum in Dublin are filled with objects, doubtless found in Ireland,

*That portion of a manuscript which records the scribe's name.

but of which the exact provenance and date are often badly established and which were not discovered in systematic excavations. On the other hand, as a result of imports and plunder, numerous Irish objects have been found in Saxon tombs in England or in Viking burials in Norway, a fact which may itself lead to further confusion. During the past few decades, however, scientifically conducted excavations have completely changed this aspect of the problem. Not alone have objects similar to those already known, been discovered in this manner, but workshops and some objects only half finished have been brought to light in almost all of the sites which have been excavated. Most striking of these finds is perhaps the little glass stud, still encased in its mould, discovered in excavations at Lagore, a find which instructs us on the method of manufacture of certain of the ornaments of the famous chalice found by chance near Ardagh in 1868. The problem of the metalwork can now be said to be solved, and this has a great bearing on that of the manuscripts.

With regard to the sculptured monuments, of which a large number is known, they belong by their very nature to the soil of the country, and, carved as they are in local stone, their native character cannot be doubted. The close similarity of their ornaments to those which decorate bronze and parchment shows the essential unity of this art whatever its medium of expression.

Let us then accept, without entering into more subtle discussion, that all which has been traditionally attributed to Ireland, does in fact belong to her. It was necessary to indicate the problem and the possible objections. We shall only return to it incidentally.

Irish art developed under unique conditions, to which it owes some of its essential characteristics. Several waves of Celtic peoples settled in Ireland at dates still uncertain. By one of these was introduced the civilization known as " La Tène ", which flourished in the regions occupied by the Celts, during the centuries immediately preceding the beginning of our era. From this time onwards, throughout the centuries, the upheavals which troubled the Continent and even reached neighbouring England, came to Ireland only as muffled echoes. Ireland (as to a large extent Scotland) escaped the Roman conquest and did not experience the barbarian invasions. However, in the fifth century, at the moment when the Roman world was crumbling, St. Patrick and his companions converted the island to Christianity, and the faith remained strongly implanted in Ireland while the Saxon conquest swept it almost completely from England. And thus it came about that Ireland found herself, more intimately perhaps than any other part of the ravaged West, in contact with the new impulses coming from the oriental monasteries.

These circumstances explain two dominant features that give to Irish art its aspect at once archaic and original; on the one hand its roots, like those of Scottish art, go back to the ancient Celtic tradition, smothered elsewhere by the Roman conquest. It represents the most perfected and definitive form of this tradition, pushing to an almost fanatical degree its taste for combinations of abstract lines, its disregard for the realistic representation of the actual world. On the other hand, it constitutes a first sketch of the Christian art of the West, very different in its coherent system from the rather indeterminate eclecticism of the contemporary arts of the Continent—a preliminary experiment which should not be ignored when the sources of the Romanesque geometricism are being sought.

But Irish art is not merely an essential record of one particular phase of an obscure past. Apart from all historical considerations, it stands out as the most satisfying and most perfect form of non-representational art which Europe has ever known, and because of this it is of immediate and burning interest for the artists of our time.

The astonishing technical perfection of this art also commands attention. The skilful hand of the artist translates the greatest subtleties of thought into patterns on metal or vellum, contriving and combining the ornaments with a versatility ever new.

This art, which was above all, however, an art of the slender line, of the line which covers and envelops a surface, was little preoccupied with problems of internal structure. It is this that led to its downfall when it was confronted by the great arts of the Middle Ages, based on a structural conception of volumes. We shall not pursue it thus far. We shall only consider its period of basic originality before the Viking invasions in the ninth century came to disturb the self-centred life of this community. The fifth and sixth centuries are as yet little known

16

and must be considered together as a time of elaboration. It is the seventh and eighth centuries and the beginning of the ninth with which we are most concerned, the period of achievement, led up to by this preparation, the period when Irish art attained a mastery which placed it in the first rank of European arts.

THE ORIGINS

THE ROOTS of Irish Early Christian art, the beginning of its development must be looked for in the art of pagan Ireland. This art is known to us intermittently, by a few outstanding objects—engraved sword scabbards, sculptured stones, jewellery—but we are little acquainted with its full history. It is nevertheless clear that it is a phase of Celtic (La Tène) art imported from the Continent and from England before the beginning of our era. It belongs to a world better known to us from allusions in later literary texts, than by archaeological remains—a world where the warrior chieftain is the essential personage, where the decoration of his dwelling, his person and his arms seems to have been the principal preoccupation of the artist.

The careful study of an object dating to the centuries immediately before Christ, such as one of the scabbards found in the Lisnacroghera crannog (fig. p. 18.) or a trumpet found near Armagh (Pl. 1), will give some idea of the quality of the decoration of that period. The ornaments engraved on the bronze sheeting of the scabbard are made of a combination of curved lines which at the same time both obey the laws of symmetry and contradict them, and which are enlivened by the insertion of small finely coiled spirals. This arrangement produces a strange harmony which both satisfy and bewilder eye and mind and leaves a vague sense of uneasiness. Little oval leaves are added to the curves of the ornament on the trumpet, binding the various elements together. This system of decoration is characteristic of La Tène art, the spirals and leaves are the disintegrated remains of the classical palmette and foliage scroll from which this art

18

developed. The continuous design composed of curves interlocking with one another in an undulating rhythm, is found at all periods of its evolution. This type of equilibrium in design achieved by a real or feigned asymmetry, is found particularly in insular ornaments, English or Irish. The decoration of a few sculptured stones in Ireland which also belong to this period, reveal a still more unyielding adoption of this method of apparent disorder, and shows to what extent Celtic art had taken root in Ireland, and how Irish artists had made it their own.

From this time on, new motifs appear in great number, side by side with the curvilinear theme, but it is this complex and sinuous system of linear combinations which is to remain the framework and the norm of Irish art,—an art which from its first beginnings preserves a taste for bewildering the beholder by its unexpected and hidden rhythms.

THE MONASTERIES

THE CONVERSION OF Ireland in the fifth century introduced a change in the patronage of art. The importance of the chieftain as client and patron of artists was obscured as his place in the organisation of the country diminished before the growing authority of the monasteries, which became the centre of all culture and all intellectual life.

These monasteries, scattered over the whole of Ireland, seem to have been at first very humble establishments analogous to the hermitages of the Egyptian desert. They consisted of a collection of cells, built of wood or of dry stone, grouped around a tiny stone-roofed chapel, usually flanked by a slab or a cross marking the tomb of the founder. The almost fierce asceticism which animated these primitive monasteries explains the humble appearance of the buildings. All artistic endeavour was concentrated in the decoration of religious objects. Some of these hermitages clung to the slopes of desolate mountains or were built on rocky islets far from the shore, settings hardly calculated to encourage great architectural undertakings.

But, little by little crowds of pilgrims and disciples invaded these hidden retreats.* The number of monks increased, the monastery became a school and sheltered a type of primitive university, and in the seventh and eighth centuries, pupils flocked to it, from an England reconverted to Christianity and from the Continent where Irish

*A text of about 800 A.D. says: " The little place where hermits settled two together, three together, are now resorts of pilgrims where hundreds, where thousands assemble."

20

missionaries were spreading the fame of their schools. Monastic cities took the place of hermitages. Occasionally, one hears of a local chieftain donating lands for the erection of new buildings; soon he will be completely overshadowed by the monks, his neighbours.

Glendalough, south of Dublin in the Wicklow mountains, offers a striking example of these different stages in the monastic life. On the steep slope overhanging one of the lakes, the foundations of the small huts of the first hermitage may still be seen. Later, probably towards the eighth century, the monastery, to allow room for expansion, was transferred lower down, where the valley, opening out, presented a level space on which many buildings could be grouped. None of them is very large; as on the Continent at the same time instead of erecting one great church, it was thought more expedient to raise several smaller ones scattered here and there. The dwellings of the monks no longer remain: made probably of wood, they have disappeared. But several churches still survive. They are built with enormous blocks of stone and their massive rectangular doorways are sometimes bordered by a band in low relief; they had (if we are to believe the indications of one of the miniatures of the Book of Kells) a heavy timber roof, covered with shingles or with ornamented leaden tiles and terminated by carved beams.* All the churches are extremely simple in plan—a rectangle, sometimes lengthened by a rectangular choir, and always without columns or pillars. A description of the church of Kildare in the seventh century evokes a picture of wooden partitions and perhaps a sort of iconostasis decorated with paintings. However, in most of the monasteries of the time, artistic endeavour seems to have been concentrated on the great sculptured crosses, ten or twelve feet in height, which stood here and there between the buildings.

These conventual establishments would probably present to our modern eyes astounding contrasts if we were enabled to visit them in their original state. A certain rusticity of appearance, a complete absence of comfort, a rather chaotic awkwardness in the disposition of the monuments were probably combined with an extreme refinement of decoration and an acute consciousness of the value of ornaments and

*One of these churches, the so-called " Saint Kevin's Kitchen ", is surmounted by a stone vault. It is probably of comparatively late date.

21

combinations of colour. In the same way, almost pagan archaisms combined in the mind of the monks and their pupils with a piety of rare quality of which contemporary religious poetry gives us a moving glimpse, and a culture far superior to that of continental monasteries of the same time. The value of this culture, which has left so little trace in texts written in Ireland, has been much discussed. But even if nothing remained but the vigorous, incisive Latin, enriched with classical and biblical references, which flowed from the pen of St. Columbanus from the time of his arrival in Gaul at the end of the sixth century, its quality could scarcely be doubted. And the fame of the Irish schools and of the wandering Irish scholars can only be explained by the exceptional standard of their teaching and the familiar usage of a culture which everywhere else had suffered too much from the uncertainty and barbarism of the times. Moreover, the image which those who knew them retained of these Irish monks, is that of scholars forever occupied in reading or in copying manuscripts. This is the picture that their English contemporary Bede gives to us every time he speaks of them. Another document, the Life of St. Columba, founder of Iona, written in the end of the seventh century by one of his successors, Adamnan, helps us to see them at work. A picture unfolds from his pages of a life where agricultural occupations necessary to the existence of the community—the care of animals, of the dairy, of the crops, etc.—are combined harmoniously with the daily copying of a sacred text or its commentary. If, in certain characteristics, in the tenderness of heart which colours all their actions and extends to the most humble of animals, the monks of St. Columba seem to us like distant precursors of the companions of St. Francis, their monasteries are not far from being, by this constant alternation of manual and intellectual activities, the forerunners of the great Benedictine monasteries of the Middle Ages.

Yet, even though they were in advance of their time, they never succeeded in completely stifling an antique past which continued to live in a transformed, but still robust manner. It is to the labours of the monks that we owe our knowledge of the pagan epics of Ireland; in the eleventh and twelfth centuries, they wrote them down and presented them as an entertainment. In the seventh and eighth centuries, this pagan world was still too acutely real to be treated so casually. But the first sketches of extraordinary themes took shape at that time; we are told of the great pagan heroes confronted by Christianity, one dying of indignation on hearing of the passion of Christ, another called from the other world by St. Patrick to help in the conversion of a recalcitrant king. These attempts to assimilate the ancient heroes show the power they still enjoyed, and to what extent the world to which they belonged was still a reality. It is not astonishing then if, not content with using the old Celtic spiral for the decoration of Christian objects, goldsmiths and sculptors sometimes mingle semi-pagan scenes with their ornaments.

Apart from the monks, was any lay power in the eighth century in a position to command the work of the artists? This is a question about which we know little. It is difficult to decide whether the great penannular brooches were worn by clerics or laymen. Some harness-mountings decorated in the same way as the ecclesiastical objects are known, and they were probably part of a warrior's equipment; in the remains of the lake-dwellings of the kings of Lagore, several metal plaques have been found, similar in technique and design to the religious art. That is about all one can say at present. Christian tombs in which the body is interred without ornaments or weapons cannot help in this respect. There remains the fact that the descriptions of the Viking invasions in Ireland in the ninth century give countless pictures of the raiders swooping down on the monasteries, smashing shrines and books, doubtless for the sake of their metal ornaments, but have merely a passing reference to the destruction of royal residences. The monasteries seem therefore to have been the chief patrons of the arts. It was through them that almost all the new ideas which profoundly altered the art of the pagan period were introduced into Ireland, and it was by them that these novelties were amalgamated and woven into a new formula.

THE PERIOD OF ELABORATION

(From the fifth to the middle of the seventh century)

IF WE NOW attempt to follow the development of this art in its various phases, we come first of all to a period—from the fifth century to the middle of the seventh—in which the sequence of styles remains obscure. It is far from being the "archaeological hiatus" it has been sometimes designated, but it can only be considered as a whole without attempting, in the still very fragmentary state of our knowledge, to give precise dating to the objects.

The art of this period is characterised by a series of diverse borrowings which come to incorporate themselves in the old Celtic decoration and are slowly absorbed into it. None of them obtrudes itself strongly enough to alter the style profoundly, but the slightly hesitating character of certain works is probably due to this diversity of inspirations.

In the first place, Ireland did not entirely escape Roman influence. As a result of trade or plundering expeditions to the coast of England, Roman objects were introduced into Ireland in much greater numbers than has been hitherto believed. Some of these objects were imitated by Irish workmen, and, more surprising still, Irish craftsmen seem to have adopted many of the techniques familiar to Roman metalworkers and enamellers. Also, with the Picts of Scotland, near neighbours of the Romans, as intermediaries, some Roman types, such as brooches, pins, etc., reached Ireland already half transformed.

It was, however, immediately before its final collapse that Roman art had its profoundest and most lasting influence on the art of Ireland,

24

and that by means of St. Patrick and his companions. St. Patrick grew up in Roman Britain. Texts (evidently later in date, but which relate a more than plausible tradition) depict him as bringing to Ireland all kinds of religious objects as well as artisans capable of manufacturing others. These objects probably typified the blend of Roman and Oriental forms which characterised the art of the first centuries of Christianity. It is more than likely that he also brought manuscripts with him: it is hard to imagine a missionary without his collection of sacred texts from which he would comment to his new converts. At any rate his biographers speak specifically of " books ". We shall probably never know definitely where these books had been copied or whether their pages were ornamented. But from the importance rapidly assumed in Irish manuscripts by decorated capitals, it can be inferred without much possibility of error that some of them were written in Italy where ornamental initials appear at an early date. They were obviously Latin texts—the Gospels and probably the Psalms.

Everything, however, in the art of this period, was not of Roman origin. Oriental elements played a considerable part in it, and we have seen that these elements probably left their mark on some of the objects brought by St. Patrick. In Ireland, they were of particular importance, due no doubt to the close contacts which the Irish monasteries seem to have maintained with the very earliest monastic foundations, those of the Near East, especially of Egypt and Syria. Though it is likely that certain Oriental motifs arrived in Ireland by indirect route—and that seems to be the case with certain types of crosses, cross-in-circle, Greek cross, etc. found engraved on Irish slabs exactly as they are to be seen on grave slabs in Gaul and Italy—in other cases, for example that of the manuscripts, there was probably more direct transmission. How then have these Coptic or Syrian manuscripts, no doubt utterly unintelligible to an Irish monk, how have they found their way to Ireland? Was it perhaps because of the attractiveness of their design and ornament? Or were they in the possession of those Oriental monks, Egyptian, Byzantine, Armenian, whose death in Ireland is recorded in Irish martyrologies? It is to them we owe the " carpet-page " which was to become one of the most characteristic features of the Irish books (Pl. 9, 18, etc.). It was they also who suggested to the Irish painters the

25

use of the interlace which they were to combine unceasingly with the spiral.

The decoration of the objects which survive from this obscure epoch retains something of the eddies and conflicts of these diverse currents and of the different ways in which they influenced the traditional art.

They are mainly metal objects, very simple, generally of gilt or silvered bronze. This taste for brilliant and colourful material is manifested still more by the use of enamel. Champlevé enamelling, an old Celtic technique, probably unknown to the Romans until they came in contact with the Gauls and the Britons who were masters of the art, must have reached Ireland very early. Several of the objects dating before the Christian era found at Lisnacroghera, in the north of Ireland, carried enamel. A fort in the south of Ireland, Garranes, which was occupied during the fifth and sixth centuries A.D. and has yielded some mediterranean pottery, and the Lagore crannog which is slightly later, both contained remains of enamellers' workshops. The fragments of multicoloured glass found at Garranes by Professor Ó Ríordáin show that already in the fifth century " millefiori " decoration of gallo-roman origin had come to be used together with the ordinary champlevé technique.

Almost all the objects of this period, penannular brooches, dress-fasteners, pins, etc., come from Roman prototypes. To these must be added hand-bells of bronze perhaps of Coptic origin, which became in Ireland, together with the crozier, the insignia of episcopal and abbatial authority, and also bronze lamps in the shape of large hanging-bowls, whose Irish origins, so long denied seems daily more probable as a result of fresh discoveries (Pl. 3, 6). The ornament on all these objects is frequently confined to very small surfaces, the extremities of the open ring of the brooches, the discs which hold the suspension hooks of the lamps. The design consists of slender spirals, sometimes arranged in trisceles, whose coils frequently terminate in a tiny animal head (Pl. 4). The oval leaf, uniting two curves, already noted, often appears in the décor. The design is always harmonious, and covers the surface pleasingly, if not very strikingly.

Nevertheless, a few works stand out from the main body of artistic production by their technical perfection as well as by their ornament.

26

First there are gold objects decorated with filigree work, one of them found at Lagore, the other in the fort of Garryduff (Co. Cork), excavated by Professor M. J. O'Kelly. The Lagore object comes from the foundations of the crannog, which were packed with the rubbish gathered from older habitation sites and must therefore be older than 650, the date of the oldest recorded occupation of the crannog. It is a little plaque of gold with a very simple interlace pattern. The Garryduff object, found in the lower level of the fort, probably goes back to a similar date. It is a tiny gold bird (half an inch long), decorated with minute spirals, possibly made to be fastened onto cloth or leather. The use of filigree, unknown to Celtic craftsmen, was most probably, like millefiori work, borrowed from the jewellery of Roman times.

Then there are some bronze objects ornamented with thin raised lines, admirable in the boldness of the curves used in their decoration: a disc found in the Bann and three bronze horns found in Cork. Even more wonderful are the fragments which, re-mounted in a perhaps arbitrary way, are known as the " Petrie crown " (Pl. 2). Enamelling appears only in the form of red blobs at the centre of the motifs. The patterns stand out in sharp, well-defined relief on the soft curve of the cone and the concave surface of the discs. The lines unfold with perfect balance to finish in a small bird head.

A brooch found in the crannog of Ardakillin, near Strokestown (Co. Roscommon) (Pl. 7b) has another variety of curvilinear pattern, modelled in high relief this time, and accompanied by a wide, ribbonlike interlacing. This interlace and that of the gold object from Lagore show the introduction into Irish ornament of new elements which we shall meet again in the manuscripts.

It is clear that already at this period the texts copied by the Irish scribes were enhanced with some ornament. A mutilated copy of the psalms preserved in the Royal Irish Academy, the " Cathach ", traditionally ascribed to St. Columba, seems to date, from the nature of the text and script, if not exactly from the time of the saint (end of the sixth century), at any rate from the beginning of the seventh century. Each psalm commences with a capital letter executed in pen and embellished in red and yellow; the majority of the capitals are surrounded by red dotting, a very striking detail, for this type of framing, of Coptic origin, was used in the West at this time by Irish scribes only. The body of the letter is formed by a system of curves, often joined by little leaves, and here and there ending in animal heads. There is nothing in the design which we have not encountered before, and these quite simple illuminations fit in very well with the decorations in metal (Pl. 7, 8).

But, on the whole, we are here dealing with a quite humble manuscript. Other books make it pretty obvious that a more complex decorative system had already been introduced into Irish scriptoria. But to find them, we must turn our attention to the Irish foundations on the Continent. St. Columbanus, having travelled over Burgundy and Switzerland, ended his life at Bobbio, south of Milan, in the first years of the seventh century. The house which he founded there maintained for a long time close relations with Ireland. Manuscripts which go back to the half-century following the foundation of the monastery are now in the Ambrosian Library in Milan, and the character of their script shows a strong Irish impress; in fact some of them were obviously brought from Ireland. Furthermore, their decoration contrasts sharply with that of contemporary Italian manuscripts. By study of these manuscripts we are enabled to see what was being done in Ireland at the time when St. Columbanus left it.

Side by side with capitals more complex than those of the Cathach, but similarly adorned with spirals, animal heads and dotting, an astonishing novelty appears. This consists of an entire page completely given over to ornament (Pl. 9), clearly of Coptic origin in its composition—very close to that of Egyptian bindings of the sixth century in which a broad ribbon interlacing forms the central motif. Here we have already the essential dispositions of the " carpet-page ", as we shall meet it later in the Book of Durrow. The colours are more varied than in the Cathach: green has been added to the red and yellow, and occasionally purple accompany them.

The ornaments incised or sculptured in low relief on the pillars and slabs which flanked the monastic oratories, correspond to these designs on metal and parchment. Here again, the ornament is reduced to a few simple lines. Spirals, knots and fretwork motifs group themselves

28

above or around a simple Latin cross or a Greek cross in circle. The stone is not usually shaped to a regular outline; a flagstone or monolithic pillar, it retains an absolutely uncompromising ruggedness, in which the crude block can still be discerned. Occasionally, as for example on the Reask pillar, the most perfect of these monuments (Pl. 10), the decorated surface is not even levelled, and the ornament adapts itself to the inequalities of the stone. This contrast between the crudity of the scarcely trimmed material and the slender, almost threadlike lines which cover its surface, gives great spontaneous charm to these monuments.

THE FIRST FLOWERING

(Late seventh—early eighth century)

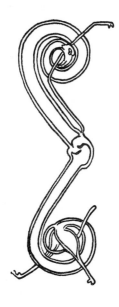

FROM THE MIDDLE of the seventh century onwards, this art, hitherto hesitant and stumbling, makes astonishing progress. Perhaps impulses derived from contacts with the outside world play some part in this transformation. England, restored to Christianity partly by Irish missions and partly by those sent from Rome, no longer formed a barrier between Ireland and the rest of the world. The Irish monks now move to and from the Continent without restraint and bring back from their journeys new ideas and at the same time a remarkable certainty in their own methods. Moreover, with the arrival in Ireland of a steadily growing throng of pupils for the Irish monks, monastic cities come into being, which provide a more propitious milieu for the development of imposing art forms than did the primitive hermitages.

The slabs and pillars which were sculptured in the second half of the seventh century bear the mark of this new environment. They are no longer untrimmed blocks, but monuments of definite form—generally great sheets of stone from five to seven feet in height, frequently surrounded by a border in low relief. Some of them resemble the page of a manuscript translated into stone, but a new idea of structure begins to be appearent. The great rectangular slab tends to take the shape of a cross. At first, there is merely a suggestion of this, and the arms appear only as slight protuberances on the sides. Soon, however, the sculptor will dare to depart from his self-imposed limits, and will model in the shape of a cross the great slab he is decorating.

New motifs appear. Either, as for example on three of the slabs on Inishkea north, spirals and a Greek cross in a circle cover almost the entire surface (Pl. 11), or interlacings are used, at times very simple, as on the large slab on Caher Island and on that at Killaghtee, at times more assured, and forming a cross as on another slab discovered on Inishkea north. These interlacings come probably from the same Coptic origin as some elements of the decoration of the Bobbio manuscripts. Another novelty is more remarkable: on several of these slabs human figures appear. They are essentially simplified, reduced to a few lines which suggest human beings without depicting them. There are also representations of the Crucifixion, with the sponge and lance bearer on either side of the nude figure of Christ (Duvillaun and Inishkea north).

All these works are engraved rather than sculptured, and the question arises as to whether they were brightened with paint. This would have made perfectly legible a design which, otherwise is decipherable only during the short periods of the day when the sun illuminates it obliquely.

Two monuments surpass all the others in the wealth and fullness of their ornament. These are the cross at Carndonagh, in Donegal, and the slab which stands about twenty miles further south in the cemetery at Fahan Mura (Pl. 12, 13, 14). Both of them are ornamented with large cruciform motifs, composed of the plaits, knots and twists of a broad ribbon. Both have human figures, very schematic, drawn in a few decorative lines. But the Carndonagh cross, by the combinations of these very simple elements achieves a grandeur and harmony hitherto unknown. This cross is accompanied by two small pillars carved on all sides. They carry figures with large rounded faces amongst whom can be recognised Jonah issuing from the whale, David playing the harp and an ecclesiastic holding a crozier and a bell. If we add to these the figures carved on the cross we have an important collection of iconographic imagery which demonstrates the new preoccupations of the Irish sculptors. But a panel of spirals similar to those on Inishkea links this monument closely to the preceding group.

Animals also appear in the ornament: a bird holding a fish in its claws on one of the pillars, and, on the cross, two groups of birds in a triscele arrangement.

This impressive cross is closely related to one of the most famous of the Irish manuscripts, the Book of Durrow, in its choice and dispositon of patterns and in their sharp definition. It is particularly enlightening to approach the manuscript after having examined the cross and the group of slabs.

The Book of Durrow contains in its pages the most perfect masterpieces of this unfolding Irish art. It is a copy of the Gospels preceded and followed by the canons of concordance and by summaries of the text. It is preserved in the Library of Trinity College, Dublin, to which it came in the seventeenth century, having belonged for centuries to the monastery founded by St. Columba at Durrow, in the centre of Ireland. As in the case of many other manuscripts, the place where its text was copied and illuminated is unknown. It seems to have been written for one of St. Columba's foundations, perhaps that of Durrow itself. The relationship of its decoration with that of the monuments at Fahan Mura and Carndonagh, however, would rather seem to point to the nearby monastery of Derry.

The text itself is a rather pure Vulgate, but the most recent researches have shown that, contrary to what has often been said, it is derived from a version of St. Jerome's text different from that which provided the model for the Northumbrian scribes. However, the accessories of the Gospels: prefaces, summaries, symbol order, go back to a tradition older than the Vulgate. There is a perfect unity and continuity about the decoration of the book. Each Gospel begins with the Evangelist's symbol drawn in the middle of the page on a field of plain vellum framed in a border of interlacing (Pl. 15, 16). Then come two pages facing each other:* on the left, a carpet-page entirely covered with ornaments and opposite, the first page of the text beginning with a monumental capital (Pl. 17, 18). The letters which follow the large initial are in ornamented characters on a background of dotting. On a more magnificent scale, it is the same composition as in the Milan manuscript. The beginning of the book includes several illuminated

*Except for the Gospel of St. Matthew, where the carpet-page has been lost.

pages and the canons of concordance of the Gospels are framed in narrow borders of interlacing, while each important paragraph of the summaries begins with a decorated letter surrounded by red dotting.

Three colours only are used throughout the manuscript, an orange-toned red, a vivid green and a beautiful golden-yellow. Another colour, now a faded brown, appears only on a few pages. Some of the capitals are filled-in in yellow and stand out from a brilliant background of red dotting, but the carpet-pages contain the three colours in almost equal proportions, often distributed in a peculiar manner on successive segments of the same interlacing and standing out in wonderful harmony against a uniform background sometimes of sepia-toned ink and sometimes the ivory surface of the parchment itself.

The distribution of the ornamental motifs is as regular as that of the colours. The broad ribbons twisted into plaits and circular knots play an important part in all the carpet-pages and in the borders which surround the symbols of the Evangelists while the capitals are mainly composed of thread-like interlace and of finely-coiled spirals, linked together by a flourish of coloured curves. Spirals appear only once on the carpet-pages, but on that occasion they cover an entire sheet. In the Book of Durrow there is only one motif not hitherto met with in Irish art. It appears on one page only—the carpet-page which precedes the Gospel of St. John—and its unusual character suggests that we are dealing with a new importation. It consists of a combination of fantastic little animals whose elongated bodies are interwoven like the ribbons of an interlace (Pl. 18). The close relationship of this design to the animal interlacing of Anglo-Saxon and Merovingian jewellery has often been stressed. It is not surprising that an Irish illuminator should have had Saxon objects in his possession, and should have imitated them. What is more striking is the coherence and vivacity which he gave to animals that were lifeless and inert on his models. Starting from an almost amorphous system of animal-headed ribbons, he seemed to create a race of tiny skipping monsters with biting jaws and flexible limbs, which he combined not in a confused meander, but following a regular and intelligible rhythm.

In doing so he subjects them to the general style of the manuscript.

The dominant impression on turning the pages of the book, is, in fact one of harmony, of calm and measured equilibrium, which nevertheless does not exclude a note of untamed strangeness which unobtrusively permeates all the decoration. This strangeness comes particularly from the deliberately abstract, obstinately inhuman character of the design. It is a mental game which delights in meanders, in disconcerting equivalences of form and colour. There is no attempt to illustrate the text, or to decorate it with reminiscences of known forms of foliage, birds or architecture. The design of the symbols which tyrannises the living form and reduces it to a series of planes and arabesques is significant in this respect (Pl. 15). The rectangular body of the symbol of St. Matthew is as far from any attempt at actual representation as are the personages on the Carndonagh cross. The lion and the eagle are quite as unreal as the beasts of the animal interlacing, and the very cohesion of the latter, the attempt of the artist to portray them as possible beings although never seen, further accentuates the feeling of a world on the borders of reality which these ornaments impart.

These tendencies are equally strongly marked in the decoration of the Carndonagh cross and the Fahan Mura slab. By means of these works, an art until then somewhat wavering, achieves for the first time full expression.

The appearance of Saxon animals in the Book of Durrow leads us to an examination of what was happening in Britain. When England again became Christian territory, close contact was established between Irish and English art and so many cross currents of influence were set up that it is sometimes difficult to distinguish what belongs to one island or to the other. It is, however, of very little importance to succeed in doing so. The composite style which, in this uncertainty, we tend to call " insular " had its roots in this early development of art which we traced in Ireland and is an intrinsic part of Irish art. The Book of Lindisfarne itself, derivative as it is, can only be understood when restored to its Irish background.

The Irish missions in England were based on a few monasteries to which quite normally, books, painters and craftsmen came from Ireland. Around the year 635 one of them was founded at Lindisfarne.

We shall come back to this later. About the same time, another was established in Suffolk at the request of the king of East Anglia, by the Irishman Fursa. Irish enamellers, no doubt, worked there and are probably responsible for a few technical anomalies (such as the use of millefiori glass) in the Anglo-Saxon objects of the Sutton Hoo tomb. It is through them also that came the enamelled bowls of purely Irish style which were found in the royal cenotaph. Eventually, by a normal process of exchange it is from such monasteries as these that Saxon objects decorated with animal interlacings were probably sent to Ireland where manuscript painters and jewellers imitated them.

These monasteries kept in close contact with Ireland where their English pupils were sent to complete their education. Thanks to Bede the history of several of them is fairly well known. The figure of Egbert dominates them all. He arrived in Ireland in his youth before 664 and was still there in 716. Others joined him, Willibrord amongst them, who arrived when he was twenty years old and after twelve years of studies left about 690 to evangelise Frisia. He took with him eleven companions, Saxons mostly, but some of them probably Irish. He founded in Echternach (Luxembourg) a monastery which remained in contact with both Ireland and Northumbria during the thirty or forty years following its foundation. Manuscripts from the Echternach library are now preserved in the Bibliothèque nationale in Paris and in a few German libraries. Those which go back to the time immediately following the foundation of the monastery present, as one might expect, a decoration of very definitely Irish character. The great Gospel-book of the Bibliothèque nationale may have come from Ireland. Its style proceeds clearly from that of the Book of Durrow. Spirals and interlacings compose its whole repertory, which does not include any animal-interlacing, but the wide ribbon-interlacing is mostly replaced by a network of fine threads which covers the surface of the large capitals, together with incredibly finely coiled spirals. The outline of the capitals is somewhat dry and academic. The symbols of the Evangelists, however, specially the great bounding lion, show a boldness of drawing, a feeling for movement quite alien to the slightly static style of Durrow.

The other Echternach manuscripts have, as well as spirals little animal heads and sometimes birds, which belong to a new stage of Irish decoration of which the Lichfield Gospels and the Lindisfarne Gospels give practically contemporary versions, one from Ireland, the other from Lindisfarne. The exact relationship between these two manuscripts is difficult to establish. They have in common the general composition of several pages and the constant use of ornament based on the weaving together of the ribbon-shaped bodies of animals and birds.

The monks of Iona founded the monastery of Lindisfarne at the request of the king of Northumbria and for nearly thirty years it was the centre of an intense missionary activity in the north of England and the Midlands. In 664 it ceased to depend directly upon Iona. This did not mean, however, that the ties with Ireland were broken. King Alfred of Northumbria, who reigned up to 705, had been a pupil of the Irish schools and remained in friendly contact with his master, Adamnan, abbot of Iona.

But meanwhile, in 674 and 680, Benedict Biscop, an English monk, founded twin monasteries in Wearmouth and Jarrow which he deliberately oriented towards mediterranean and Continental influences. He made several journeys to Gaul and Italy in search of masons, manuscripts and icons. What the masons did, we only know imperfectly and the surviving fragments of the churches of the two monasteries give the impression of rather poor constructions. But the Codex Amiatinus, which is a copy, made in one of the two monasteries, of manuscripts brought from Italy, has come down to us. Its text is very pure Vulgate. Its illuminations are as remote as possible from Irish art. The painters of Lindisfarne knew about these novelties and drew on them up to a point. The thorough training in abstract methods of decoration which they had received from their Irish masters had, however, become so strongly ingrained that it took a long time to die out.

The various stages of this evolution have left their mark in the manuscripts which belonged to the library of Lindisfarne. These manuscripts were brought to Durham in the tenth century when the monks, fleeing before the Viking raids, ended their long wandering by establishing there a new monastery. Some of them are still in the library of the cathedral of Durham. The best known of all, the Book of Lindisfarne, is now in the British Library.

The oldest of these manuscripts, which is in Durham (Ms. A.II.10), by its decoration of wide ribbon interlacings painted in red, green and yellow, to which is added a bright blue, brings us back to a style contemporary with that of the Book of Durrow or perhaps slightly earlier. Dr. Nordenfalk is inclined to think that it may have been written in Lindisfarne, but it may also have been brought over from Ireland towards the middle of the seventh century—a few years after the foundation of the monastery. Another (Durham, Ms. A.II.17) appears as a development of the Durrow style. Its only surviving capital is of very large size, like those of the Echternach Gospels, but its surface is partly covered by combinations of little beasts with long snouts akin up to a point to those in the Book of Durrow. At the beginning of the Gospel of St. Mark there is a Crucifixion, instead of the symbol of the Evangelist. The shape of the cross is reminiscent of that on the Duvillaun slab, but the figure of Christ is clothed in a sort of ribbon drapery.

As for the Lindisfarne Gospels, it has been deduced from the colophon that it was made about the year 700 or a little later by a Saxon abbot of the monastery called Eadfrith. Mr. Bruce-Mitford holds the view that illuminations and text are by the same hand, which is possible. In this case, the Irish character of the illuminations would be explained by more than a simple persistence of the Irish tradition in Lindisfarne, as it seems that Eadfrith was one of these Saxon students who completed their education by a stay in Ireland. That he knew some of the manuscripts, Italian and Byzantine, which Benedict had brought back from Italy is made obvious by the text itself, which is very close to that of the Codex Amiatinus and by the semi-realistic style of the portraits of the evangelists and the imitations of Greek inscriptions which accompany them. All the rest of the decoration of the manuscript proceeds from the current Irish repertory, though it is handled with a certain amount of stiffness very different from the imaginative treatment of the painter of the Book of Durrow. But, with this reservation, the sumptuous pages of the Book of Lindisfarne represent both a continuation of the style of the Book of Durrow and a new stage in the development of Irish decoration. There is the same scheme of carpet-pages and of decorated initials. The carpet-pages, however, have become so complex that the eye, at first, cannot disentangle from the rich display of lines and colours the tracery of animal and bird bodies or the meanders of infinitely fine threads in the interlacings. The initials have become such majestic ornaments that they cover almost the whole page with their flowerings of spirals and knots. It is the same arrangement, but much more elaborate. The colours are basically the same as in the earlier manuscripts, red, green, yellow, blue, purple, but, by a device used already by the painter of the Echternach Gospels, there are at least two tones for each, so that there is a whole range of varying shades, with a preponderance of purple, green, pink and mauve. Though the decorative elements are the same as in the Book of Durrow, animal interlacing, which made only a fleeting appearance there, plays here, as in Ms. A.II.17 an essential part. It is composed of little beasts with slim heads, sometimes vaguely akin to greyhounds, of birds with gorgeous feathers and of strange creatures half quadrupeds, half birds. If these animals are less remote from reality than those of the Book of Durrow, their decorative treatment is still conditioned by the tendencies to illusionism, to optical deception, which are fundamental features of Irish art. This persistence of method illustrates the extraordinary hold which such a system had on the minds of the painters, orientating them mercilessly towards an ideal of abstraction (Pl. 19, 22, 23).

The Lichfield Gospels are closely related in many ways to those of Lindisfarne, though they are less stiff in appearance, more spontaneous, and in this way much nearer to the true spirit of Irish art. The text is of the type, with Vulgate readings side by side with Old Latin ones, which became common in Ireland towards the end of the seventh century. Originating no doubt in an Irish scriptorium, it was given, in the late eighth century, to a Welsh monastery, and then it came to the cathedral of Lichfield where it is now kept. It has the same animals and the same birds as the Lindisfarne Gospels, but they are caught up in an impetuous rhythm very different from the reasoned pattern of the art of Lindisfarne. The frames around the first lines of the text are made of the contorted bodies of animals. The Evangelists are represented by

38

their portraits and their symbols on the same page. But these portraits, differing in attitude from those of the Book of Lindisfarne, have nothing of their realistic appearance and follow wholly the abstract approach of Irish art. Their clothes have become a combination of ribbons and geometric patterns. St. Mark's chair is made of two emaciated animal bodies, tied up in the knots of their tails and tongues; and the symbolic lion—a near relation of that in the Echternach Gospels—jumping from one to the other, adds yet another fantastic element, completing the transformation of a representational theme into an ornamental one (Pl. 20, 21).

Thus the Lichfield Gospels appear as a prelude to the development of the art which we shall find displayed in the eighth century on the high crosses and on the metal objects. Its comparative inaccessibility in a cathedral treasury and the poor state of preservation of its illuminations have prevented it from taking so far the place it deserves as a much more vivid and original manuscript than the well preserved but very academic Lindisfarne Gospels.

THE APOGEE

(Eighth century, beginning of the ninth)

WITH THE EIGHTH century Irish art reaches a technical perfection allied to a skill and virtuosity in decoration which would be astonishing at any period, but which are particularly striking at this stage of the early Middle Ages. It is true that our knowledge of it is very fragmentary but the few objects and monuments which have survived suffice to give an idea of its signal quality. Metal, sculpture and illumination developed with equal brilliance and in each technique we have masterpieces—the Ardagh Chalice and Tara brooch, the Ahenny crosses, the Book of Kells.

METALWORK

For a long time archaeological data on eighth century metalwork was of the vaguest and it was necessary to turn to the tombs of Norway (fairly well-dated) for any precise information: an object looted from Ireland and interred in the tomb of a Viking who died in the first half of the ninth century was necessarily anterior to that date and belonged probably to the eighth century.

But the excavations carried out by Dr. Hencken, at Lagore crannog to the north of Dublin, have added considerably to our knowledge of the metalwork of this period. They have produced a collection of metal objects, going back for the most part—according to historical data—to the end of the seventh or to the eighth century. Moreover, the crannog contained workshops; numerous crucibles for bronze casting were found there, and fragments of bones, carved with small panels of animals or interlacing, which were probably used to prepare the moulds for decorative bronze plates. Small flat stones were also found, covered with rough sketches of the decorative motifs common in Irish art. This type of sketch occurs elsewhere also, and the ruins of one of the buildings of the monastery of Nendrum, in the north of Ireland, have yielded similar drawings. But at Lagore, they have the added interest that one of the designs thus outlined, is met with again at the centre of a spiral on one of the bronze objects found in the excavation—a belt buckle which was probably cast by the bronzeworkers of Lagore and of which we have here a first sketch (Pl. 29). In another part of the crannog we can almost see the glass-makers at work. A level which is dated at latest to the beginning of the eighth century has produced a series of tiny moulds of baked clay, destined for the manufacture of glass studs. One of these moulds has a splash of blue glass on its edge; another still contains the stud which it served to cast. It is a small circular boss decorated with a sunken geometric design. Bosses of similar manufacture form part of the decoration of quite a large number of Irish metalwork objects. Sometimes they are used just as they left the mould; some, such as the two human heads on the Tara brooch, are miniature masterpieces. In other cases the sunken groove is afterwards filled with glass of a different colour. The latter technique may be noted on two small beads of blue glass ornamented with a red circle, on the Tara brooch, and on some of the glass plaques of the handles and the foot of the Ardagh chalice.

Thus, the finds from Lagore lead us quite naturally to the mention of a few of the most remarkable objects of eighth century metalwork, and confirm their dating to the beginning of the century, a chronology which their decoration would in any case suggest.

A certain number of large brooches, derived from the penannular brooches of the preceding period have been found in Ireland and in Scotland. In most cases these are in fact long pins furnished with a decorative ring which often reaches three to five inches in diameter. They are generally made of gilt silver or gilt bronze and they are decorated with deeply cut patterns imitated from the chip-carvings of the Saxon and Continental arts of the migration period, though probably produced by casting. They are frequently adorned with glass or amber studs mounted in fairly high relief and sometimes with small panels of filigree.

One of these, the " Tara brooch " which is far from being the most imposing in size, surpasses all the others in the fineness of its ornament and the diversity of techniques employed in its manufacture. It was discovered near the mouth of the Boyne and had probably been brought there as Viking loot* (Pl. 27, 28, 29). The ring is made from a bronze plaque decorated on one side with finely modelled chip-carving-like motifs of gilt bronze and sheets of metal carrying a spiral-pattern so thin that it may have been etched by an acid. On the other side (Pl. 28), the bronze plaque is divided by raised borders in which ornamental panels of gold filigree and amber bands are held. This is the side intended to be seen habitually and it has an almost baroque brilliance. The whole effect is of a glistening play of lines and colour, and on both sides, studs of patterned glass and of carved amber add a further element of brightness.

Coloured splendour and unbelievable delicacy of workmanship are found in still greater perfection on the Ardagh chalice, which is perhaps a product of the same atelier. Its extremely simple structure, like that of the brooch, contributes to its imposing harmony (Pl. 24, 25, 26). It is made of two semi-spheres of sheet silver joined by a large rivet which is masked by an annular band of gilt bronze with chased ornaments; two other decorative bands surround the cup, one a little below the rim, the other on the foot. The handles, the plaques with which they are affixed to the bowl and the two medallions on either side of the globular surface of the chalice are covered with filigree work and red and blue enamels. The silver cup which at first appears perfectly plain, was engraved with a fine design in which the names of the twelve apostles in stately characters are combined with a few animal interlacings.

*It was named the " Tara brooch " by one of its first owners, from the ancient capital of the kings of Ireland in the neighbourhood of the place of the discovery—a purely fanciful appellation.

In order to assign to such an object its proper place in the metalwork of its time, it is sufficient to compare it with some of the principal pieces of Continental jewellery of the Early Middle Ages, which have either survived or which are known from reasonably accurate documents. Such works for example as the crowns found at Guarazzar in Spain, the book-cover and reliquary of the tooth of St. John in the treasury of Monza in Lombardy, the shrine of St. Maurice-d'Agaune in Switzerland, the chalice attributed to St. Eloi, which was in the possession of the abbey of Chelles, near Paris until the Revolution (known from an engraving), and the "reliquary of Pépin d'Aquitaine" preserved in the treasury of Conques in the centre of France. In all of these, studs of coloured stones protrude in very high relief from a richly ornamented background now a mosaic of coloured glass, now a network of filigree or chiselled metal. These studs have probably inspired the enamelled bosses mounted in a plaitwork of golden wire which punctuate the Ardagh chalice and the strips of glass plaques which cover its handles possibly owe something also to Continental jewellery. But there the resemblance ceases. The chalice, in its perfect harmony and the balance of its composition, so far surpasses the other objects as to seem the product of a different world. The artist who conceived it despises the exuberance and ostentation in which his contemporaries delight; he attains his effect by a delicacy of workmanship which leaves far behind the best of which they were capable. And one is forced to the conclusion that at this period, Irish metalwork held unparalleled mastery in the Christian world of the West. If now we turn to the pagan arts, Scandinavian or Saxon, of the same period, we find there a taste for variegated surfaces of chipped interlacing and in the Saxon objects, for discs of red and blue glass which probably influenced the Irish artist. But nothing, not even the wonderfully executed objects found just before the last war at Sutton Hoo approaches in excellence the Ardagh chalice, which is free from their accent of sumptuous barbarism.

We have repeatedly praised the technical perfection of its decoration. This is particularly striking in the treatment of the filigree which adorns the cup and in the manufacture of the enamels. In order to achieve an effect of more pronounced brilliance and depth the filigree is made of several gold wires of different granulations, soldered one above the other, forming interlacings or the outlines of little animal bodies of incredible fineness or the gold wire is soldered on to an openwork pattern of gold leaf (Pl. 26). As for the enamels, they represent an anomaly in the decoration of the period. They are not cloisonné like the Byzantine enamels, which indeed were never imitated by the Irish at that time. Neither are they champlevé enamels such as we find on other Irish objects. They are evidently made according to a very old Celtic method of which we find examples at an earlier date in Gaulish jewellery and which consists of moulding the enamel in a small mould of clay fitted with a metal grill. The small blue glass beads, incrusted with gold spirals, which ornament the foot of the chalice and some of the glass tablets on the handles, were made by a similar process. Others, as we have seen, were made of moulded glass whose grooves were subsequently decorated.

A few objects more ordinary in fabrication, and far from attaining the perfect execution of the chalice, show other aspects of eighth century enamelling. One of these is a belt or rather a belt-shrine, which was found during the last war at Moylough, in Co. Sligo (Pl. 30, 31). Its structure is characterised by the same simplicity as that of the chalice, its framework being a band of bronze edged with two tubular borders, on which decorative panels are applied. Here again we find enamel bosses with silver insets, mounted in high relief. But the frames which surround the embossed or openwork silver plaques are filled with red and yellow champlevé enamel and with millefiori in which blue and white dominate.

A similar use of enamel is found on the great bronze hanging-bowls which continue into the eighth century the type of the sixth and seventh centuries with spiral ornamented escutcheons. We have seen that " millefiori " enamel (the application of small cubes cut from a rod of patterned glass, to a sunken field of bronze) was a Gallo-Roman technique introduced into Ireland at an early period as is shown by the presence of a rod of millefiori glass at Garranes. Similar glass rods found at Lagore, reveal the same work in progress in an eighth century workshop. One of these bowls taken to Norway by a Viking is now in Bergen Museum (Pl. 33). Its base is ornamented with a large star

44

pattern, on whose silver field shine yellow, blue, red, white and green. The chains for suspension were held in place by small human figures whose bodies are rectangles of enamel and millefiori, and whose large round heads, modelled in relief, were probably cast by *cire perdue* technique.

Semi-spherical heads of a similar type strike a singular note on a plaque of openwork bronze representing the Crucifixion, found at Athlone, in the centre of Ireland (Pl. 32). This was probably part of an ornamental book-cover or else a " pax ". We find here again the same simplified human forms, the same exaggerated massive heads as on the carvings of the Carndonagh cross. But the jeweller, in modelling the heads in high relief against the flat background of the bodies covered with an embroidery of chased ornaments, has obtained a powerful effect of hieratic majesty.

Two objects of gilt-bronze, preserved in the Museum of St. Germain-en-Laye, are admirable examples at once of the skill of Irish metal casters and of the cunning virtuosity of their decoration (Pl. 34, 41). Both of these have on one face a design of large spirals swelling into raised bosses; several snake-like bodies unwind from each spiral, some reptile-headed, others ending in a human head, a bird's head or a wolf-like profile with open jaws and menacing teeth, which threatens to devour man or serpents. This is a memory of the old theme of the devouring monster, dear to Celtic mythology, where it probably represents a god of the sea; but here it is absorbed and swept along by the ornament and it chiefly serves to give a note of terror to its complex windings. The composition shows the love of asymmetrical and deceptive arrangements carried almost to a frenzy. The very shape of the object which just eludes the semi-circular, the manner in which two animal bodies provide an illusory border, are in themselves striking. But an attentive examination of the disposition of the serpent bodies reinforces this impression. At first glance three serpents appear to unfold from each of the three-centred bosses; on more careful examination, it appears that some of them are merely tangents but press so closely against the periphery of the coil that they seem to issue from it. The composition high-lights three biting beasts, but although two of them sink their fangs in a human skull, the third misses the man and

45

merely attacks a reptile. One could go on indefinitely with this analysis; everywhere one would find these assonances, giving the illusion of true rhymes, and to these arrangements the Lichfield Gospels would supply nearly exact parallels.

An enamelled crozier head found in 1954 at Ekerö, near Stockholm, during the excavation of a Swedish settlement of the early middle ages, was made, as Dr. Holmquist has shown convincingly, by craftsmen working exactly on the same lines as those who produced the St. Germain objects (Pl. 35, 36). The ornament is formed by the curved neck and head of an animal whose fierce jaws hold a human head. This is the same theme once again, but here it is probably intended for Jonah emerging from the whale. One side is bold chip carving; the other side and the knop are enamelled in red and yellow with the insertion of some millefiori. There are also glass studs on the animal head similar to some of those found on the belt and the chalice. Thus we see that the various types of ornament which have been sometimes used separately are in no way incompatible.

Many of the fragments of gilt bronze, looted from Ireland and found in Viking graves in Norway—disc brooches, mountings torn from reliquaries or shrines—show the same methods of decoration as the large objects. Small panels ornamented with an interlacing, a spiral or an animal-interlacing are each set in a frame and their network is interrupted here and there by a glass or amber stud breaking the uniformity of the surface. Often in two symmetrical compartments, analogous motifs are matched, but they are rarely identical in all details. Generally the animal is similar merely in attitude and the centres of the spirals vary endlessly.

SCULPTURE

The sculpture of this period shows for the most part a close relationship with the metalwork and is often inspired by it.

We have observed that the church doorways were very simple (Pl. 39), the decoration in stone being concentrated on the high crosses and on a few slabs. These crosses have a much more monumental character, and a more rigidly fixed architecture than the Carndonagh cross. They are no longer sheets of shaped stone raised against the sky; the contour-line has lost its undulating and slightly irregular character. The arms are firmly rectangular in design and generally emphasised by a raised moulding and are joined by a great open circle which distinguishes the Irish crosses from their English contemporaries. The imitation of metalwork models is evident in the large bosses in relief, recalling the studs which, in a metal cross, would disguise the rivets joining the two metal mountings on either side through a wooden core; the mouldings at the corners undoubtedly copy the covering of the joints between the plaques themselves.

These crosses are firmly fixed in a stone base which is often itself ornamented, but they are never definitely associated with a stone tomb, as were many of the slabs of the preceding epoch, and it is difficult to ascertain precisely what their purpose was. A schematic plan of a monastery preserved in the eighth century Book of Mulling, shows a circular enclosure around which crosses are disposed according to the cardinal points, four dedicated to the Evangelists, four to the great Prophets, while inside the enclosure are found others, dedicated to Christ and the Apostles, to the Holy Spirit, etc. They seem to play the role of guardians, protecting the monastery from the evil powers which threaten it from the four corners of the world.

Those crosses which still remain in their original position seem to have been placed around the principal church. They are imposing monuments, often more than ten feet high. The whole surface is covered with a network of ornament cut in the level surface of the stone so as to stand out from the background in a uniform relief. The only accents are marked by the mouldings and the circular bosses. But these few stresses in the relief are sufficient to give them an architectural structure which completely distinguishes them from the earlier slabs. From whatever angle you look at them, they offer to the eye elaborate combinations of mouldings which give them a monumental appearance. The ornament is sometimes divided into panels and sometimes runs freely over the surface. They are in the main the same motifs as we have met on the metalwork, but their chronological distribution is nevertheless of great interest.

These crosses seem in fact to fall into two groups; the one, which belongs to the first half of the eighth century has foliate spirals, with animal heads, very similar to those of the Book of Lindisfarne or the Tara brooch, accompanied by angular motifs or thread-like interlacings, but animal interlacing rarely occurs. The crosses of this group are found mainly on the borders of the great plain of the south of Ireland, not far from Cashel, at Ahenny (Pl. 37, 38), Kilkieran, Killamery, etc. and also further north at Lorrha, and the cross at Dromiskin, near Dundalk is closely related to them. The other group, which belongs to the neighbourhood of the monastery of Clonmacnoise, near Athlone, is a little later in date; the principal monument, the Bealin cross was erected by an abbot of Clonmacnoise who died in 810 or 811 (Pl. 49, fig. p. 40). The spirals here are of a more complex type mingled with interlacings as we shall find them on the Book of Kells, and animal interlacings arranged in a scroll play an essential role.

Side by side with the ornamental patterns, some of the crosspanels carry figured scenes. These are of two different types. On the bases or at the extremities of the arms of several crosses are representations of biblical scenes—Adam and Eve, Noah calling the animals into the ark, the sacrifice of Abraham, the three young men in the fiery furnace, etc. The figures are elementary, but the scene is none the less legible, and there one finds a totally new preoccupation with safeguarding the intelligibility of the subject. These scenes belong in the main to a series of examples of the aid given by God to his chosen people, which are found at a very early date in Christian art. Their presence on these crosses points to an attempt to bring Irish art into step with that of Christianity in general, an attempt already apparent in the Carndonagh sculptures and which becomes more and more marked in the succeeding centuries, until it comes to a full development in the great figured crosses of the ninth and tenth centuries. But the fact that, in the present examples, these scenes are more or less relegated to the extremities of the monument shows that this tendency is still very much in its initial stages. The cross at Moone (Kildare) where some of these scenes cover a monumental base may mark the transition to the figured crosses.

Other scenes remain much more difficult of interpretation, and these are incorporated more spontaneously in the ornamental style. On the cross of Bealin (fig. p. 40), on a slab from Banagher now in the National Museum (Pl. 46), and on a pillar from Clonmacnoise, we find a rider hunting the stag, a stag caught in a trap, still another rider and a dragon, and a series of dragons devouring one another. The fact that one of the riders carries a crozier seems to indicate that these scenes are clearly Christian. They have some parallels in Scottish carvings, which have probably the same character. The stag plays an important part in primitive Christian symbolism but it has an equally essential role in Celtic mythology, and the presence on the Clonmacnoise pillar of a figure with crossed legs in the traditional attitude of the Deer-God of the Celts, suggests the possibility that we have here an adaptation of pagan representations to which a new significance has been given. The very ease of the composition, the way the figures are arranged in an intertwined pattern confirms the impression that here there is no question of a recent importation. The Bealin panel is particularly striking from this point of view (fig. p. 40). The repetition of the same conventional attitude for the horse and stag produces a strange rhythm and the entanglement of the dog, which is itself standing on the horse's head, with the legs of the stag, assures a continuity of line which makes of the whole design a sort of interlace.

On the base of the Ahenny cross an enigmatic story unfolds itself. Here again there is an archaic aspect, although it comprises undeniably Christian elements. A group of ecclesiastics bearing croziers is likely to be meant for the Mission of the Apostles. But the other scenes are strange: one shows horsemen and a chariot, another a man among many animals and the third the funeral of a headless body. These panels cannot represent, as sometimes suggested, the funeral of a king of Cashel, as the same funeral scene is depicted in an abridged form far away on the cross at Dromiskin, near Dundalk, where the first episode shows a stag hunt, and similar chariots appear on other crosses. It seems rather to be again the adaptation of traditional pagan figurations to a new Christian meaning.

ILLUMINATION

Decorated manuscripts must have formed an essential part of Irish art in the eighth century and the beginning of the ninth. But even more than metalwork, they have suffered from pillage and destruction, so that we possess only a few fragments from what must have been a veritable treasury of painted vellum. After the Lichfield Gospels which must belong to the very early years of the century, the two principal books of the eighth century—the Gospel-book No. 51 in the Library of St. Gall and the Book of Mac Regol in the Bodleian Library at Oxford—probably represented the more ordinary level in illumination. One dates to the middle and the other to the second half of the century (the painter-scribe Mac Regol died in 820). We are led to believe that others of superior quality in design must have existed beside these everyday productions, by the few manuscripts which survive from the beginning of the ninth century. Some, which can be grouped around the Book of Armagh, are illustrated by very fine pen drawings, another, the Book of Kells, surpasses them all by the fullness and dazzling richness of its decorations.

The library of the monastery founded by St. Gall, one of the companions of St. Columbanus, and which has taken his name, includes a certain number of Irish manuscripts, some written by Irish monks at St. Gall, others brought from Ireland at various times. The latter is probably the case for the Evangeliary No. 51. It is an abundantly decorated book, whose somewhat massive style recalls the Athlone crucifixion and the decoration of the enamelled bowls. Unlike most of the great Evangeliaries of the earlier period it has only one carpet-page (Pl. 42) which faces the Chi-Rho of St. Matthew's Gospel. Each Gospel opens with a portrait, but a novelty which had already appeared in the Durham Gospels, here takes more importance; at the end of the Gospel of St. John, there are two pages representing the Crucifixion and the Last Judgement. The treatment of the figures throughout the manuscript, shows a striking tendency to transform faces and garments into decorative motifs. The drapery which envelopes the crucified body of Christ is reduced to a few wide ribbons twisted in a coloured whirl (Pl. 45). The garments of the Evangelists (Pl. 44) are merely a series of almost symmetrical curves which form a fine coloured design with little relation to actual drapery. The intensity of the colours—blue, red, yellow, green—adds still more to the strange appearance of the figures, on which they are distributed without the slightest attempt at versimilitude.

The Gospel-book illuminated and transcribed, according to the colophon, by Mac Regol, abbot of Birr in Offaly, belongs in many repects to the same style. Mac Regol however, allows himself to be carried away in a sort of decorative loquacity, which is not without eloquence, but which leads him sometimes to neglect details and does not escape disorderliness (Pl. 43). Other volumes of smaller format—the Book of Dimma, the Book of Mulling—are in reality pocket editions of this type of book. They contain the same portraits of the Evangelists in frames of ornaments, the same unrealistic treatment of human figures. This style still survives in the beginning of the ninth century, delicate in design, clothed in harmonies of rose and yellow, in the decoration of the Stowe manuscripts in the library of the Royal Irish Academy.

The existence, side by side with this, of another more imaginative style, related in its fertile fantasy to that of the Lichfield Gospels, is indicated by a group of manuscripts, decorated with pen drawings of astonishing elegance and vivacity, which belong to the beginning of the ninth century. One of them is the famous volume which contains a copy of the New Testament and texts concerning St. Patrick—the Book of Armagh (Pl. 47). The colophon describes it as a copy made by Ferdomnagh, a scribe of Armagh, under the dictation of the abbot Torbach who governed the monastery of Armagh for only a few months in 807-808. Two copies of the Grammar of Priscian a little later in date are very close in style; one, made in Ireland, was brought to the Continent by an Irishman fleeing from the Viking raids and it is now in the Library of St. Gall; the other, probably the work of a refugee Irishman already on the Continent, has come into the possession of the Library of the University of Leyden. In all these manuscripts we find decoration of a wonderful elegance, in which all the usual motifs of Irish ornament, birds, quadrupeds, spirals, stylised human figures are woven and entwined with astonishing verve around the framework of the letters (Pl. 48).

Strange as it may seem this rather slight decoration leads us quite naturally to that of the Book of Kells, which has, as well as the

51

sumptuous pages which make it one of the most impressive manuscripts of the Middle Ages, a profusion of small initials composed of intertwined beasts and men, whose agility and continually renewed inventiveness recall, though with a much more impetuous quality, the Book of Armagh and the Priscians (Pl. 48, 50, 51, 53).

Kells is not far from Armagh and the two monasteries seem to have had close contacts with each other which would easily account for these similarities.

But the history of the Book of Kells is a complicated one and to understand it fully one must take into account that the foundation of the monastery at Kells was a direct result of the exodus of the monks from Iona. The monastery of Iona, although located on the coast of Scotland, remained during the seventh and eighth centuries peopled by Irishmen and was the mother-house of all St. Columba's Irish foundations. Nevertheless it did not appear in Scotland as a lone monastery isolated in a milieu of opposing traditions, but rather as the most thoroughly Irish focus in a large and profoundly Hibernicised region. All Scottish art of this period is impregnated with adaptations of Irish elements, and the stone crosses of Iona and of the neighbouring island of Islay are Irish in their form and Scottish in certain features of their decoration, which include spirals and interlaced bosses swollen into semi-spheres.

Iona was one of the first victims of the Viking raids. The Irish annals recall that in 801 it was sacked by the " Gentiles "—the pagans from Norway. Two years later the Iona monks secured a site for a monastery at Kells, to the south of Armagh and a little to the north of the future site of Dublin. In the years immediately following, a monastery was built and the monks abandoned for the time being the too exposed island. This tragic exodus finds an echo in a marginal note in the Book of Armagh, which was being copied by Ferdomnagh at that very time.

It is difficult to know whether the Iona monks brought with them, as well as the other objects mentioned in the history of their flight, the already partly decorated Book of Kells, but it seems more than likely that they did. However, the work was doubtless continued in the new monastery as the analogies with certain initials in the Book of Armagh

52

seem to indicate. It will perhaps always be impossible to establish the dividing line between what was done in either monastery and it really does not matter very much if we don't succeed in doing it as Iona and Kells were really one and the same monastery.

The Book of Kells is of quite a different order of sophistication from the preceding manuscripts and the designs of certain pages are of such exquisite ingenuity that their decoration must have taken years. It remained unfinished. Mr. A. Friend once attempted to prove that all the decoration of the great pages was done at Iona, and spoke of " the destruction of the great scriptorium of Iona " by the Vikings. This is going rather too far. We know that quite a large number of monks were massacred during the second attack on the island; to assume an utter annihilation, when manifestly the surviving monks were actively instigating the erection of the new church at Kells, is to put too great a strain on credibility. One can imagine only, that part of the decoration was already completed when the monks left Iona and probably continued with many stops and starts due both to the uncertainty of the times and to the various attempts made by the monks of Kells to return to their island metropolis. It is more likely that far from disappearing overnight, the scriptorium degenerated by degrees—deprived of its best artists by those repeated flights to the Continent of which we have many proofs.

We have clear proof that vigorous artistic effort manifested itself at Kells from the founding of the monastery, in the oldest of the sculptured crosses which remain in the cemetery at Kells—that which is designated by an inscription on its base as the cross "of Patrick and Columba " (Pl. 55). Its ornament, with the exception of a foliage scroll, belongs to the ordinary repertoire of Irish art; but the spirals are raised in semi-spheres as on the crosses of the Iona group. The ornament is combined with a number of figured scenes depicting Christian subjects and this insistent interest in iconography is also one of the striking characteristics of the Book of Kells.

Kells therefore appears as the direct successor of Iona and the book must have been continued in an atmosphere very little different from that in which it was begun—fundamentally Irish in tradition but open nevertheless to the influence of Continental models.

These diverse aspects help to explain the complexity of the Book of Kells. In it we find, particularly on the great initial pages, Irish ornament carried to a frenzy of intricacy and abstraction. Spirals of fantastic fineness flow over the great Chi-Rho page in a dizzy efflorescence (Pl. 40). Their centres become tiny filigreed birds' heads, or twist into knots. Sumptuous brocades are woven of the folded and bent bodies of men and birds, whose heads, hands and plumage enhance, here and there, the continuous network (Pl. 52). Throughout the whole text unimaginable combinations of elongated animals and of acrobatic figures twine themselves around the capitals, enlivening each page with multi-coloured tones (Pl. 48, 53). The first letters of the Lucan genealogy of Christ are joined together right down the page by a garland in which the painter seems to have become gradually intoxicated by the perpetual movements created by his brush. He begins by coiling tiny beasts around his letters, then the letters themselves are transformed into agile beings which are bent to their shape. Sometimes fantastic plants are added to the more habitual motifs. These are probably a sign of new borrowings.

The Book of Kells does indeed betray a current of new trends such as Irish art had not known since the end of the seventh century. This outside influence does not show itself quite so suddenly; nothing cuts across the general style of the manuscript in the way that the Evangelists of Lindisfarne oppose the ornamental pages which accompany them. Everything is incorporated in a general rhythm. The borrowing stops at the subject or at the disposition but does not in the least affect the exigencies of the style. The sources of outside inspiration are none the less manifestly numerous. The Iona-Kells scriptorium evidently possessed or borrowed foreign decorated manuscripts. In the years which led to the Carolingian renaissance, some of them must have been imposing works. Mr. Friend has shown the kinship of the first pages of the canons of concordance, with their arcades and the symbols above the references to the corresponding gospel, with the canons of a Carolingian Evangeliary of about 800. Although the conclusions which he has drawn from this cannot be accepted wholesale, the fact is nevertheless quite obvious. The representation of the Virgin and Child surrounded by angels (Pl. 57) was probably inspired by Coptic models. The last page of St. Mark's gospel with its elongated lions, is very close to a page of an Essen manuscript. The great number of capitals made from intertwined animals recalls the Sacramentary of Gellone. Sometimes there is obvious imitation, sometimes a common inspiration. The Book of Kells comes from a scriptorium infinitely more conversant with the fashions of the time than those which produced the Ms. 51 of St. Gall or the Mac Regol Gospels.

A clear tendency to illustrate the text is constantly apparent. The St. Gall Gospels already had two large pictorial pages, but the Temptation of Christ and the Arrest of Christ (Pl. 54) in the Book of Kells are much more strictly an illuminated commentary on the written word. Innumerable details in the small designs which fill the intervals of the text are its literal or symbolic commentary. This perhaps is partly the reason why some of them are animated with a spirit of genuine observation which is altogether new and which gives a note of unexpected realism.

This immense work, this entire world of ornaments and personages is certainly not due to a single painter. An attentive examination will show the imprint of different hands, the diverse treatments of ornaments each corresponding to its own colour-scheme. The manuscript is probably the product of an entire scriptorium engaged on it for quite a long period. This scriptorium was doubtless responsible for other manuscripts of comparable virtuosity and the Bobbio Gospel-book, which almost completely disappeared in the burning of the Turin library, was probably brought from Iona or from Kells to Italy's Irish monastery. With some divergencies of style it shows the same richness in design and the same taste for a lyrical abundance of ornament.

CONCLUSION

With the ninth century, the great creative period of Irish art comes near its end. On the one hand, the confusion which resulted from the Viking invasions, and on the other the attraction of Continental models—first Carolingian and then Romanesque—contributed to the destruction of the fragile combination of circumstances which was responsible for its flowering and which determined its originality.

The illuminators, fleeing before the invasion, emigrate to the Continent. Nevertheless, the great crosses of the ninth and tenth century display a striking version of Carolingian art combined with traditionally Irish motifs. A vivid and often disconcerting form of Romanesque decoration flourishes in the twelfth century side by side with metalwork of mixed Scandinavian and Irish styles whose products are often very effective.

But none of this is comparable with the rare phenomenon of which we are witnesses in the seventh and eighth centuries—the creation of a completely original artistic formula. It is not merely the more or less successful product of skilful craftsmen and inventive decorators, but rather a new conception of the artist's relations with the universe.

It was this, undoubtedly, that almost unconsciously inspired the many Continental illuminators who turned to those insular models, attempting to appropriate the secret of a decoration which obsessed them. Geneviève Micheli has shown the extraordinary adventures of the Irish style in Merovingian and Carolingian illumination, the surge of this tide of interlacing and fantastic animals which breaks on the Continental scriptoria and results in the most varied and surprising adaptations. Quite often it is only the mannerisms of this style, its purely superficial characteristics that are imitated and transposed. Certain adaptations are " in the manner of " to the point of caricature.

But more than this, something of the method which directed the organisation of this art, of the attitude of mind which governed its elaboration, must have penetrated by means of itinerant Irish masters into Continental scriptoria. Did it thus play a part in the elaboration of

Romanesque sculpture whose roots are to be found in the illuminations of the early eleventh century? Focillon and Kingsley Porter claim that it did. Geneviève Micheli has pointed to one of the possible transmission routes, which would lead from the scriptorium of Tours to that of Limoges and to the great Aquitanian manuscripts of the eleventh century—the cradle of the Romanesque sculpture of south-western France.

If such a transmission is probable, it is not merely as the stereotyped repetition of forms which in themselves have only an accessory significance. Romanesque art is full of interlacings, of intertwined beasts which could be either Oriental or Irish in origin. What matter; these are only the ingredients, in themselves inert. The living, animating force which Irish art, like some Oriental arts, only to a greater, more coherent degree, had to offer to the Continent was a manner or reconciling these elements, a method for creating them, a formula which permitted further elaboration. It is not necessarily when the Romanesque artist is drawing the windings of an interlace that the spirit of the decorator of the Carndonagh cross or of the Book of Kells is most alive in him. It is rather when, taking a human figure, he refuses to accept it as such, but with an authoritative hand, bends and twists it to follow the exacting lines of an ornament or the curve of a capital, or indeed when he stretches it out in vertical rigidity in the jambs of a doorway. The " statue-colonne " might well be the final result of this age-long reflection on the sway of the artist over a world docilely subject to his law. And the sketches of Villard de Honnecourt, which offer us so many recipes for torturing the human form, contain perhaps a last echo of the teaching of the Irish masters.

What can we really know of their system? It was based as that of all abstract arts, on a refusal of reality. The jewellers, illuminators and sculptors of Ireland were above all preoccupied with combinations of lines and colours whose rhythms pleased them. Their art is sometimes pure plastic dialectics, an intellectual exercise which owes nothing to the outside world. The flowing lines of interlacings, combinations of curves, satisfy them with their harmonious tracery. But more often still, it is acrobatics on the border of reality. A repertoire appears of strange forms which suggest plants, animals, human beings—a whole world parallel to ours and which, nevertheless, has its own rules—a world of singular creations, which the artist bends, spins out and interweaves at will, where in a moment, by a mysterious insinuation, a form passes to another form and unobtrusively becomes different.

In all this, reality plays no part. It is the idea of the animal, of the animal recreated according to the fantasy of the mind, which is the essential. It is the idea also of the human being, and then neither the proportions nor the usual appearance of man have any importance. Only the minimum of identifying features remain—a face, arms, the suggestion of the body and the feet. Within these essential contours, the sinuous line, coiled or interwoven, holds absolute sway. Thus to use the word "caricature", the word " clumsiness ", so often applied to these strange representations, is to reason from wrong premises.

Moreover it is not only the reality of living forms which the Irish artist is constantly skirting without ever adopting. There is another reality, abstract however, which seems both to attract and repel him. It is that of geometric forms. The spiral, the circle, the square, are like so many mirages which he perpetually conjures up and which vanish as soon as we attempt to examine them. For centuries, the Irish artist played with the spiral, drawing it out, unfolding it, embellishing it with leaf patterns and animal heads, mingling it with interlacings and swelling it into a semi-sphere, but never allowing it to become static and to decay into a purely mathematical coiling of lines. When, eventually, in the tenth century, the artist, too preoccupied with other problems, stopped for a while this play of variations, the spiral, becoming rigidly geometric, very soon vanished from his repertoire. So too with the circle which is suggested and hinted at by a group of interlacings. To make a perfect circle would only require breaking and reuniting the thread of the weaving in two or four places. The Copts have done this and later the Arabs, but the Irish scarcely ever. And the always slightly oblique weaving of the threads of the interlace forms irregular lozenges, figures with curved sides, but very rarely squares. The fear of absolute symmetry which we have several times remarked on and the many subtle detours used in avoiding it are part of the same trend.

For their decoration then, the Irish of the eighth century created a fictitious world, a dream of a pliant and malleable universe, which, by skilful treatment and by constant acrobatic feats, they maintained at an equal distance from these two quite opposite dangers—realism and geometry—thus preserving to the greatest possible extent its unreal character.

We shall perhaps never be able to assess how much survives, in such a conception, of very ancient prehistoric beliefs, and to what extent the artist who acts in this manner is the successor of the magician, master of beings and of natural forces, who was his distant ancestor. But Irish epic in which the mainspring of the action is provided rather by *geasa*—magical interdictions—than by psychological reactions, introduces us probably to a world familiar also to the artist. On these ancient data, elaborated into a reasoned discipline far removed from the dark impulses of the primitive, was built up an artistic system, at once subtle, coherent and harmonious in its strangeness, and this labyrinthine dream, this disciplined effervescence of the imagination, have never ceased to haunt and to trouble those who, in the course of the centuries, have met them face to face.

BIBLIOGRAPHY

ABBREVIATIONS
J.R.S.A.I.   Journal of the Royal Society of Antiquaries of Ireland.
P.R.I.A.   Proceedings of the Royal Irish Academy.

ORDNANCE SURVEY LETTERS
The first systematic researches in the field of Irish archaeology were those made for the Ordnance Survey in 1835/41. The letters which passed on this occasion between John O'Donovan, Thomas O'Connor, George Petrie, etc., remain an inexhaustible source of information. Roneotyped copies of them are deposited in several libraries.

GENERAL
George PETRIE, *The Ecclesiastical Architecture of Ireland anterior to the Norman Invasion,* Dublin, 1845.

George PETRIE, *Christian Inscriptions in the Irish Language* (ed. Margaret Stokes), 2 vols., Dublin, 1872, 1878.

The Earl of DUNRAVEN, *Notes on Irish Architecture* (ed. Margaret Stokes), 2 vols., London, 1875, 1877.

Margaret STOKES, *Early Christian Art in Ireland,* London, 1887, Dublin, 1911, 1928.

G. COFFEY, *Guide to the Celtic Antiquities of the Christian Period preserved in the National Museum, Dublin,* Dublin, 1910 (second edition).

Arthur C. CHAMPNEYS, *Irish Ecclesiastical Architecture,* London, 1910, Dublin, 1975.

R. A. S. MACALISTER, *The Archaeology of Ireland,* London, 1928 (first edition).

R. A. S. MACALISTER, *Corpus Inscriptionum Insularum Celticarum,* 2 vols., Dublin, 1945, 1949.

Françoise HENRY, *Irish Art in the Early Christian Period,* London, 1940, 1947; enlarged and revised edition, 1965, followed by: *Irish Art during the Viking Invasions,* 1967.

Harold G. LEASK, *Irish Churches and Monastic Buildings*, vol. I: *The First Phase and the Romanesque*, Dundalk, 1955.

M. and L. de PAOR, *Early Christian Ireland*, London, 1958.

L. BIELER, *Ireland, Harbinger of the Middle Ages*, London, New York, Toronto, 1963.

The Course of Irish History (ed. T. W. Moody and F. X. Martin), Cork, 1967.

SCULPTURE

Henry S. CRAWFORD, *Handbook of Carved Ornament of the Early Christian Period*, Dublin, 1926.

Arthur Kingsley PORTER, *The Crosses and Culture of Ireland*, New Haven, 1931, New York, 1971.

Françoise HENRY, *La sculpture irlandaise pendant les douze premiers siècles de l'ère chrétienne*, 2 vols., Paris, 1932.

Eric H. L. SEXTON, *A Descriptive and Bibliographical List of Irish Figure Sculpture in the Early Christian Period*, Portland (Maine), 1946.

METALWORK

Christian Art in Ancient Ireland, vol. I (ed. Adolf Mahr), Dublin, 1932; vol. II (ed. Joseph Raftery), Dublin, 1941.

Jan PETERSEN, *British Antiquities of the Viking Period found in Norway*, vol. V of: *Viking Antiquities in Great Britain and Ireland*, Oslo, 1940.

Treasures of early Irish Art, 1500 B.C. to 1500 A.D. (catalogue of exhibition in New York, etc.; Texts by various authors, catalogue by G. Frank MITCHELL), New York, 1977.

MANUSCRIPTS

G. J. WESTWOOD, *Fac-similes of the Miniatures and Ornaments of Anglo-Saxon and Irish Manuscripts*, London, 1868.

S. ROBINSON, *Celtic Illuminative Art in the Gospel Books of Durrow, Lindisfarne and Kells*, Dublin, 1908.

E. Heinrich ZIMMERMANN, *Vorkarolingische Miniaturen*, vols. III, IV, Berlin, 1916.

E. A. LOWE, *Codices Latini Antiquiores,* vol. II, *Great Britain and Ireland* (Oxford, 1935), and *passim* in other volumes.

Geneviève L. MICHELI, *L'enluminure du haut Moyen-Age et les influences irlandaises,* Brussels, 1939.

F. MASAI, *Essai sur les origines de la miniature dite irlandaise,* Brussels, 1947.

Carl NORDENFALK, *Irish and Anglo-Saxon Manuscripts,* London, 1977.

Besides these general indications, it has seemed useful to give a few references more specifically connected with the subject matter of each chapter:

Introduction
Henri FOCILLON, *L'art des sculpteurs romans,* Paris, 1931.

Dom Fernand CABROL et Dom Henry LECLERCQ, *Dictionnaire d'Archéologie chrétienne et de Liturgie,* Paris, 1907 sqq; see art.: *Irlande.*

The Origins
Eoin MAC NEILL, *Phases of Irish History,* Dublin, 1919.

Thomas F. O'RAHILLY, *Early Irish History and Mythology,* Dublin, 1946.

M. HERITY and G. EOGAN, *Ireland in Prehistory,* London, 1977.

J. Romilly ALLEN, *Celtic Art in Pagan and Christian Times,* London, 1904.

Ian FINLAY, *Celtic Art, an Introduction,* London, 1973.

The Monasteries
William REEVES, *The Life of St. Columba, Founder of Hy, written by Adamnan* (text and commentary), Dublin, 1857.

A. O.–M. O. ANDERSON, *Adamnan's Life of Columba,* London, 1961.

Dom Louis GOUGAUD, *Les Chrétientés celtiques,* Paris, 1911 (English translation: *Christianity in Celtic Lands,* London, 1932).

J. F. KENNEY, *The Sources of the Early History of Ireland,* vol. I: *Ecclesiastical,* New York, 1929; revised edition (L. Bieler), 1970.

Robin FLOWER, *The Irish Tradition,* Oxford, 1947.

Rev. John RYAN, S.J., *Irish Monasticism, Origins and early Development,* Dublin, 1931.

Kathleen HUGHES, *The Church in early Irish Society,* London, 1966.

Tomás Ó FIAICH, *The Monastic Life in early Christian Ireland,* Capuchin Annual, 1969, p. 116.

Ludwig BIELER, *The Life and Legend of St. Patrick,* Dublin, 1949.

Saint Patrick (Thomas Davis Lectures), ed. Rev. John Ryan, S.J., Dublin, 1958.

Liam PRICE, *Glendalough, St. Kevin's Road* in: *Essays and Studies presented to Professor Eoin Mac Neill,* Dublin, 1940. p. 244.

Harold G. LEASK, *Glendalough, Co. Wicklow,* Dublin, 1951.

The period of Elaboration

Seán P. Ó RÍORDÁIN, *Roman material in Ireland,* P.R.I.A., 1942 (C), p. 77.

Colloqium on Hiberno-Roman Relations and Material Remains, (September 1974), P.R.I.A., 1976 (C), p. 171.

R. A. G. CARSON and Claire O'KELLY, *A Catalogue of the Roman Coins from New Grange, Co. Meath,* P.R.I.A., 1977 (C), p. 35.

Seán P. Ó RÍORDÁIN, *The Excavation of a large earthen Ring-Fort, at Garranes, Co. Cork,* P.R.I.A., 1942 (C), p. 77.

M. J. O'KELLY, *Two Ring-Forts at Garryduff, Co. Cork,* P.R.I.A., 1937 (C), p. 17.

Charles THOMAS, *Imported Late-Roman Mediterranean Pottery in Ireland and Western Britain: Chronologies and Implications,* P.R.I.A., 1976 (C), p. 245.

E. T. LEEDS, *Celtic Ornament in the British Isles down to A.D. 700,* Oxford, 1933.

T. D. KENDRICK, *British Hanging-Bowls,* Antiquity, 1932, p. 161.

Françoise HENRY, *Hanging-Bowls,* J.R.S.A.I., 1936, p. 209.

C. S. M. WALKER, *Sancti Columbani Opera,* Dublin, 1957.

Margaret STOKES, *Six Months in the Appenines in Search of Irish Saints in Italy,* London, 1892.

Margaret STOKES, *Three Months in the Forests of France, a Pilgrimage in Search of the Vestiges of Irish Saints in France,* London, 1895.

Carl NORDENFALK, *Before the Book of Durrow*, Acta Arch., 1947, p. 141.

Françoise HENRY, *Les débuts de la miniature irlandaise,* Gazette des Beaux-Arts, 1950, p. 5.

The First Flowering

BEDE, *Historia Ecclesiastica Gentis Anglorum,* in: *Venerabilis Baedae Opera Historica* (ed. Plummer), Oxford, 1896; revised edition forthcoming.

Book of Durrow: *Evangeliorum Quattuor Codex Durmachensis,* Olten, Lausanne, Fribourg, 1960, vol. I: facsimile, vol. II: Text by A. A. LUCE, G. O. SIMMS, P. MEYER, L. BIELER.

Eric G. MILLAR, *The Lindisfarne Gospels,* London, 1923.

Book of Lindisfarne: *Evangeliorum Quattuor Codex Lindisfarnensis,* Olten, Lausanne, Fribourg, vol. I (1956): facsimile, vol. II (1960): Text by T. D. KENDRICK, T. J. BROWN, R. L. S. BRUCE-MITFORD, H. ROSEN-RUNGE, A. S. C. ROSS, E. G. STANLEY, A. E. A. WERNER.

Françoise HENRY, *The Lindisfarne Gospels,* Antiquity, 1963, p. 100.

T. D. KENDRICK, *Anglo-Saxon Art,* London, 1938.

Nils ÅBERG, *The Occident and the Orient in the Art of the Seventh Century,* Part I: *The British Isles,* Stockholm, 1943.

The Apogee

Hugh HENCKEN, *Lagore Crannog, an Irish Royal Residence of the 7th to 10th Centuries A.D.,* P.R.I.A., 1950 (C), p. 1, including (pp. 18-32): Liam PRICE, *The History of Lagore, from the Annals and other Sources.*

Françoise HENRY, *Irish Enamels of the Dark Ages and their Relation to the Cloisonné Techniques,* in: *Dark Age Britain* (ed. D. B. Harden), London, 1956, p. 71.

Liam S. GOGAN, *The Ardagh Chalice,* Dublin, 1932.

R. M. ORGAN, *Examination of the Ardagh Chalice, A Case History in Application of Science in Examination of Works of Art* (ed. W. J. Young), Boston, 1973.

M. J. O'KELLY, *The Belt-shrine from Moylough,* J.R.S.A.I., 1965, p. 149.

Françoise HENRY, *Deux objets de bronze irlandais au Musée des Antiquités nationales*, Préhistoire, 1938, p. 65.

W. HOLMQVIST, *An Irish Crozier-Head found near Stockholm*, Ant. Journ., 1955, p. 46.

R. B. K. STEVENSON, *The Hunterston Brooch and its Significance*, Medieval Arch., 1974.

G. L. MICHELI, *Les manuscrits de St. Gall et de Reichenau*, Revue Archéologique, 1936, I, p. 189, II, p. 56.

The Irish Miniatures in the Abbey Library of St. Gall, Berne, Olten, Lausanne, 1954. Text by J. DUFT and Peter MEYER.

E. SULLIVAN, *The Book of Kells*, London, 1914.

Book of Kells: *Evangeliorum Quattuor Codex Cenannensis*, vols. I and II: facsimile, vol. III: text by E. H. ALTON, P. MEYER, G. O. SIMMS, Berne, 1950-51.

The Book of Kells, Reproduction from the Manuscript in Trinity College, Dublin, with a *Study of the Manuscript* by Françoise HENRY, New York, London, 1974.

A. M. FRIEND, *The Canon Tables of the Book of Kells*, in: *Medieval Studies in Memory of A. Kingsley Porter*, Cambridge (Mass.), p. 611.

A. WERNER, *The Madonna and Child Miniature in the Book of Kells*, Art Bulletin, 1972.

Conclusion

Arthur Kingsley PORTER, *Spanish Romanesque Sculpture, Introduction*, Florence, 1928.

Pl. 1 Detail from bronze trumpet found near Armagh (N.M.D.)

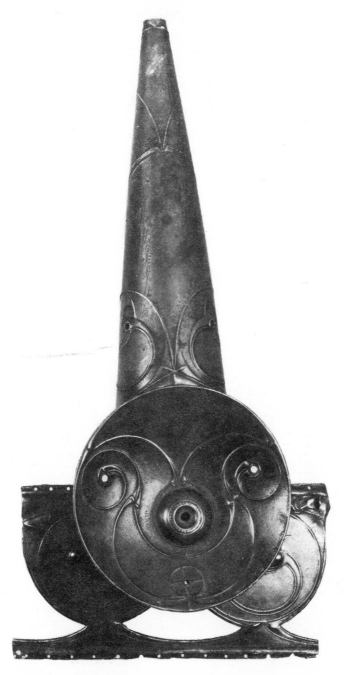

Pl. 2   The " Petrie crown " (N.M.D.) (about 1/1)

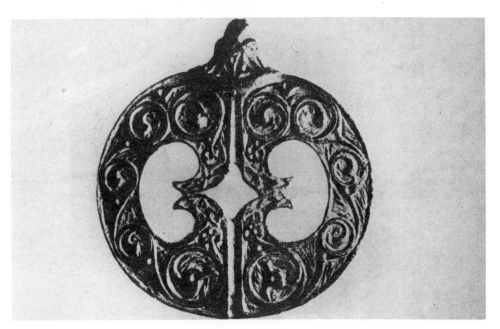

Pl. 3. *a* Openwork bronze disc from the River Bann (Ulster Mus.) (2/1)

b Detail of enamelled penannular brooch (N.M.D.) (2/1)

Pl. 4. Enamelled bronze latchet (N.M.D.) (about 2/1)

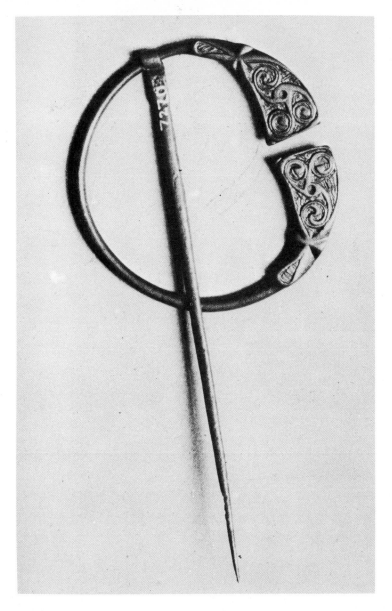

Pl. 5. Penannular brooch found in Ireland (Liverpool Museum)
(about 1/1)

Pl. 6. *a* Enamelled bronze disc found in Lagore (N.M.D.) (1/1)
b Enamelled bronze handle of hanging-bowl found in Winchester (Brit. Mus.) (1/1)

Pl. 7. *a, c* Initials from the 'Cathach' (R.I.A.)
b Bronze brooch from Ardakillin crannog (N.M.D.) (about 1/1)

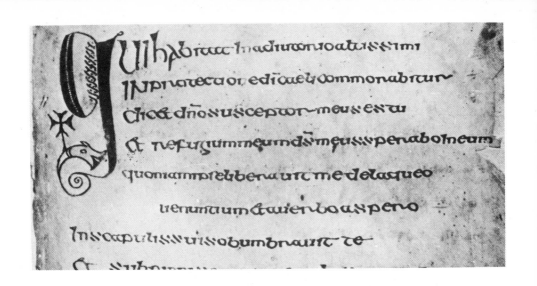

Pl. 8. *a* Initial from the 'Cathach' (R.I.A.)
b Book of Durrow, beginning of St. Luke's Gospel (T.C.D.)

Pl. 9. Manuscript from the Library of Bobbio monastery
(Ambrosian Libr., Milan, D.23 sup.)

Pl. 10.　Engraved pillar, Reask (Kerry)

Pl. 11.   Engraved slab, Inishkea north (Mayo)

Pl. 12. Carved slab, Fahan Mura (Donegal)

Pl. 13.   Cross and pillars, Carndonagh (Donegal)

Pl. 14. Carndonagh cross (Donegal) (in original position)

Pl. 15. Book of Durrow, symbol of St. Matthew (T.C.D.)

Pl. 16.   Book of Durrow, symbol at beginning of St. John's Gospel (T.C.D.)

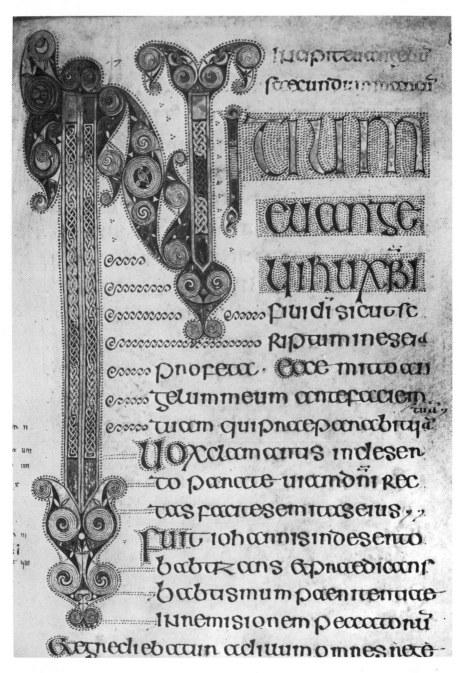

Pl. 17. Book of Durrow, beginning of St. Mark's Gospel (T.C.D.)

Pl. 18. Book of Durrow, ornamental page (T.C.D.)

Pl. 19. Book of Lindisfarne, ornamental page (Brit. Libr.)

Pl. 20. Lichfield Gospels, detail of ornamental page (Lichfield Cathedral)

Pl. 21. Lichfield Gospels, St. Mark (Lichfield Cathedral)

Pl. 22. Book of Lindisfarne, beginning of St. Mark's Gospel, detail
(Brit. Libr.)

Pl. 23. Book of Lindisfarne, beginning of St. Luke's Gospel (Brit. Libr.)

Pl. 24. The Ardagh Chalice (N.M.D.)

Pl. 25.   The Ardagh Chalice, detail (N.M.D.)

Pl. 26. The Ardagh Chalice, detail (N.M.D.)

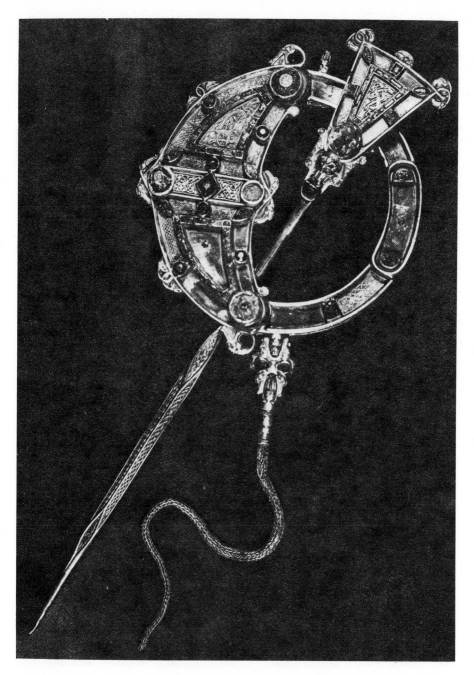

Pl. 27. The "Tara brooch"
(N.M.D.)

Pl. 28. The " Tara brooch ", detail (N.M.D.) (approx. 2/1)

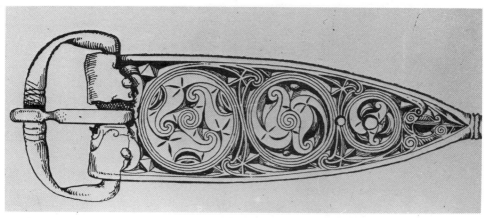

Pl. 29. *a* The " Tara brooch ", detail (N.M.D.)
b Belt-buckle found at Lagore (N.M.D.)

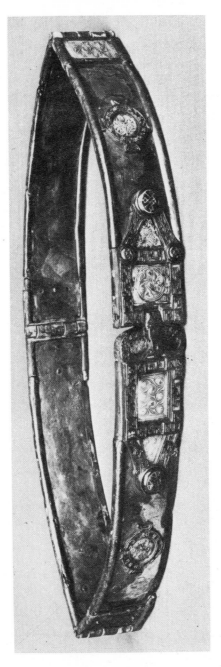

Pl. 30. Belt-shrine found at Moylough (Sligo) (N.M.D.)

Pl. 31. Moylough belt, details (N.M.D.)

Pl. 32.   Gilt bronze plaque found at Athlone (N.M.D.)

Pl. 33. Enamelled ornaments on hanging bowl found at Miklebostad
(Norway) (Bergen Mus.)

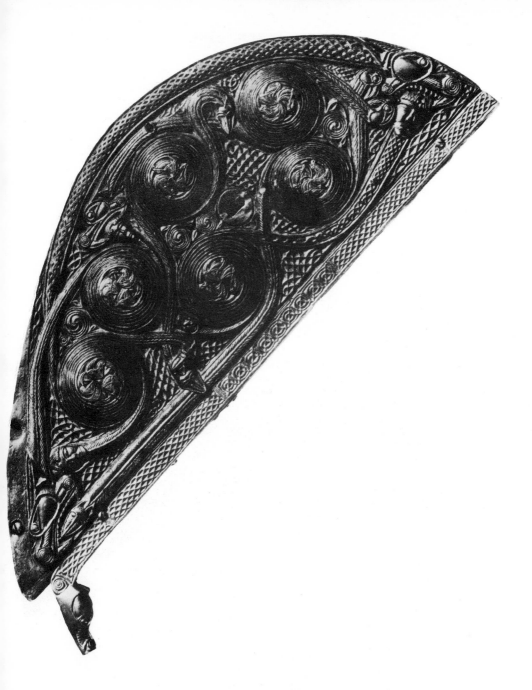

Pl. 34. Gilt bronze object (no loc.) (Musée des Ant. nationales)

Pl. 35. Detail of Irish crozier found at Ekerö (Sweden)
(Stockholm Museum)

Pl. 36. Irish crozier found at Ekerö (Sweden)
(Stockholm Museum)

Pl. 37. North Cross, Ahenny (Tipperary)

Pl. 38. South Cross, Ahenny, detail

Pl. 39. Doorway of the church at Fore (Westmeath)

Pl. 40. Book of Kells, detail (T.C.D.)

Pl. 41. Gilt bronze object, detail (Mus. Ant. Nat.)

Pl. 42.   St. Gall Gospels, ornamental page (Cath. Libr. of St. Gall, no. 51)

Pl. 43. Book of Mac Regol, St. Mark (Bodleian Libr., Oxford)

Pl. 44.   St. Gall Gospels, St. Matthew (Cath. Libr. of St. Gall, no. 51)

Pl. 45.   St. Gall Gospels, Crucifixion (Cath. Libr. of St. Gall, no. 51)

Pl. 46. Slab from Banagher (Offaly) originally from Clonmacnoise
(N.M.D.)

Pl. 47. Book of Armagh, symbol of St. Mark (T.C.D.)

Pl. 48. *a* Book of Kells, capital (T.C.D.)
      b Book of Armagh, capital (T.C.D.)

Pl. 49.   Bealin Cross (Westmeath)

Pl. 50. Book of Kells, capitals (T.C.D.)

Pl. 51. Book of Kells, capitals (T.C.D.)

Pl. 52. Book of Kells, details (T.C.D.)

Pl. 53. Book of Kells, capital (T.C.D.)

Pl. 54. Book of Kells, Arrest of Christ (T.C.D.)

Pl. 55.　Cross at Kells (Meath)

Pl. 56. Book of Kells, canon table (T.C.D.)

Pl. 57. Book of Kells, Virgin and Child (T.C.D.)

SAOL AGUS CULTÚR IN ÉIRINN

IRISH LIFE AND CULTURE

The following booklets have been published in this series:

1. THEATRE IN IRELAND by Micheál Mac Liammóir.
2. POETRY IN MODERN IRELAND by Austin Clarke.
3. IRISH FOLK MUSIC SONG AND DANCE by Donal O'Sullivan.
4. IRISH LANDSCAPE by R. Lloyd Praeger.
5. CONAMARA by Seán Mac Giollarnáth.
6. IRISH CLASSICAL POETRY by Eleanor Knott.
7. THE PERSONALITY OF LEINSTER by Maurice Craig.
8. EARLY IRISH SOCIETY edited by Myles Dillon.
9. THE FORTUNES OF THE IRISH LANGUAGE by Daniel Corkery. (No longer available in this series.)
10. SAGA AND MYTH IN ANCIENT IRELAND by Gerard Murphy.
11. THE OSSIANIC LORE AND ROMANTIC TALES OF MEDIEVAL IRELAND by Gerard Murphy.
12. SOCIAL LIFE IN IRELAND 1800–45 edited by R. B. McDowell.
13. DUBLIN by Desmond F. Moore.
14. THE IRISH LANGUAGE by David Greene.
15. IRISH FOLK CUSTOM AND BELIEF by Seán Ó Súilleabháin.
16. THE IRISH HARP by Joan Rimmer.
17. ERIUGENA by John J. O'Meara.
18. WRITING IN IRISH TODAY by David Greene.
19. STORYTELLING IN IRISH TRADITION by Seán Ó Súilleabháin.

SPECIAL SERIES:

ART IRLANDAIS by Françoise Henry.

EARLY CHRISTIAN IRISH ART by Françoise Henry (translated by Máire MacDermott).

CROIX SCULPTÉES IRLANDAISES by Françoise Henry.

IRISH HIGH CROSSES by Françoise Henry.

IRELAND'S VERNACULAR ARCHITECTURE by Kevin Danaher.

COLONIAL NATIONALISM, 1698–1776 by J. G. Simms.

OTHER PUBLICATIONS:

PAGAN AND EARLY CHRISTIAN IRELAND: Map (99×62cm) by Patrick Scott.

MAP OF PAGAN AND EARLY CHRISTIAN IRELAND: Explanatory Notes by Harold G. Leask

IRISH CULTURAL INFLUENCE IN EUROPE VITH TO XIITH CENTURY: Map (99×62cm) by Thurlough Connolly.

IRISH CULTURAL INFLUENCE IN EUROPE VITH TO XIITH CENTURY: Key to Map by an tAthair Tomás Ó Fiaich.

W9-BIG-214

Life in the Rainforest

Plants, Animals, and People

By Melvin and Gilda Berger
Illustrated by Geoffrey Brittingham

Ideals Children's Books • Nashville, Tennessee

The authors, artist, and publisher wish to thank the following for their invaluable advice and instruction for this book:

Jane Hyman, B.S., M. Ed. (Reading), M. Ed. (Special Needs), Ed. D. (candidate)

Rose Feinberg, B.S., M. Ed. (Elementary Education), Ed. D. (Reading and Language Arts)

R.L. 2.1 Spache

Published by Ideals Children's Books
An imprint of Hambleton-Hill Publishing, Inc.
Nashville, Tennessee 37218

Printed and bound in the United States of America

Library of Congress Cataloging-in-Publication Data
Berger, Melvin.
    Life in the rainforest : plants, animals, and people / by Melvin and Gilda Berger ; illustrated by Geoffrey H. Brittingham.
        p.   cm.—(Discovery readers)
    Includes index.
    ISBN 1-57102-023-3 (lib. bdg.)—ISBN 1-57102-007-1 (paper)
    1. Rain forest ecology—Juvenile literature. 2. Rain forest fauna—Juvenile literature. 3. Rain forest plants—Juvenile literature. 4. Human ecology—Tropics—Juvenile literature. [1. Rain forest ecology. 2. Ecology.] I. Berger, Gilda. II. Brittingham, Geoffrey, ill. III. Title. IV. Series.
    QH541.5.R27B45   1994
    574.5'2642'0913—dc20   94-6006
                                                                CIP
                                                                AC

Life in the Rainforest is part of the *Discovery Readers*™ series.
Discovery Readers is a trademark of Hambleton-Hill Publishing, Inc.

What lives in the rainforest?
More than half of the different kinds
    of plants in the world live there.
Nearly half of the different kinds of
    animals in the world live there.
Millions of people live there.

3

Tall trees live in the rainforest.
Some grow as high as 100 feet.
That's as tall as a ten-story building!

The trees are covered with leaves.
They form a kind of roof over the
    rainforest.
The roof is called a canopy
    (KAN-uh-pee).
The canopy keeps out most of the
    sun's light.
This makes the rainforest very dark.

4

Most rainforests are near the
    equator.
The equator is an imaginary line
    around the middle of the world.
The area around the equator is
    called the tropics.

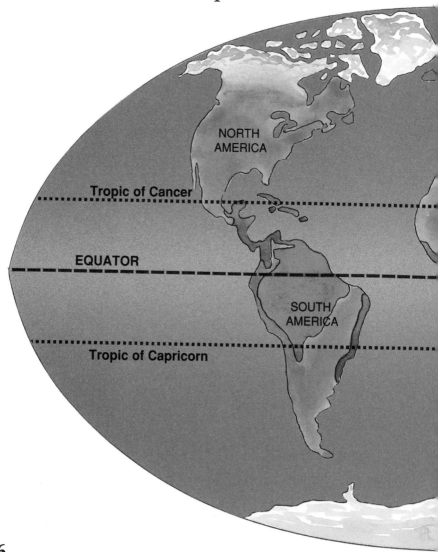

Rainforests near the equator are
called tropical rainforests.
In these rainforests every day is like
a hot summer day.

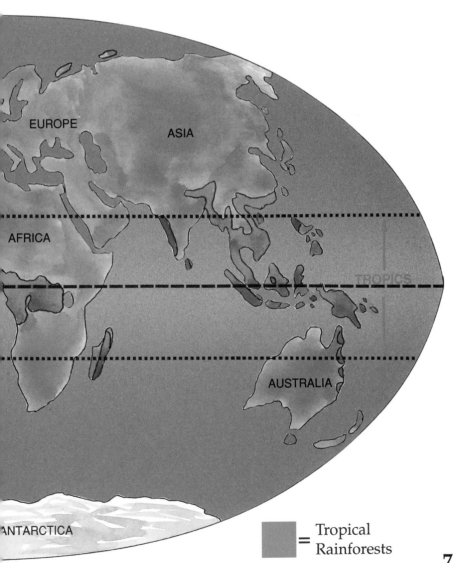

EUROPE

ASIA

AFRICA

TROPICS

AUSTRALIA

ANTARCTICA

= Tropical
Rainforests

7

Other rainforests are farther from
  the equator.
They are not as hot.
They are called temperate rainforests.

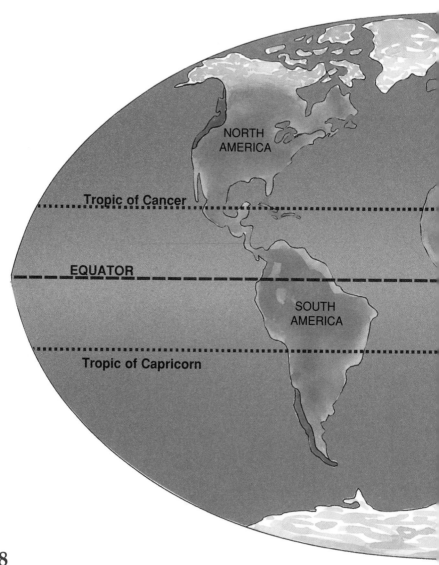

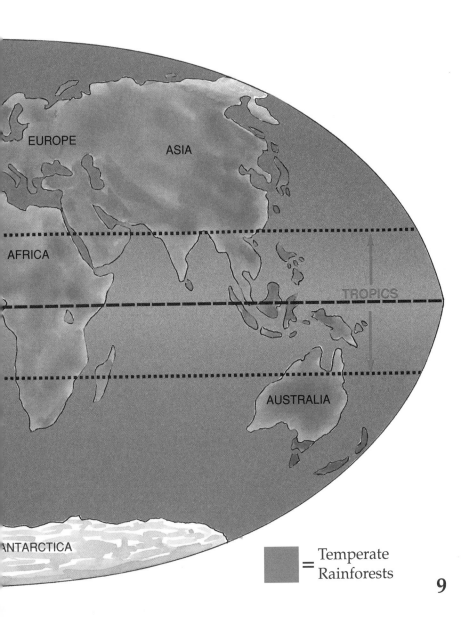

EUROPE

ASIA

AFRICA

TROPICS

AUSTRALIA

ANTARCTICA

= Temperate
Rainforests

9

All rainforests are very wet.
More rain falls in these areas than
 anywhere else on earth.
It rains for a while almost every day.

The plants, animals, and people in
this book all live in the tropical
rainforests.
The trees of the tropical rainforests
are thick and heavy.
Many animals, such as monkeys,
live in these trees.

The howler monkey is very noisy.
Its cry, "A-GOO-WAH!" rings out
through the forest.
The cry is very, very loud.
Other monkeys can hear it from two
miles away!

Rainforest monkeys have long tails.
These tails are like extra arms.
They help the monkeys swing from
    tree to tree.

Sloths also live in the trees.
They are quiet animals.
Mostly they hang upside down.
Or they move very, very slowly.

Some large animals hunt sloths.
But the sloths can't run away.
And they are too small to fight back.
So what do they do?

The sloths hide.
Or they stay very still.
Their gray fur blends in with the
    branches.
Often their enemies don't see them.

Ocelot

Sloth

Many birds also make their homes
   in the trees.
High in the canopy sits the harpy
   eagle.
The harpy is the biggest of all eagles.
It is taller than many first graders!

The harpy eats meat.
It flies fast and has sharp claws.
It also has a strong, hooked beak.

The harpy waits to see something
   move.
Maybe it spies a rat.
Down swoops the harpy.
It quickly catches the rat.

Parrot

Toucan

Parrots and toucans (TOO-kans) are
colorful birds that build nests in
the trees.
The parrots have short, strong bills.
They crack hard seeds and nuts.

The toucans have sharp, long bills.
They bite off figs and other fruits.
They also snag spiders and insects.

18

Snakes hang down from other tree
limbs.
One kind is the boa constrictor
(BOH-ah kun-strik-tor).
It is a large snake, about twenty
feet long.
This boa can stretch as high as a
two-story house!

Some big animals hide on the low
     branches.
The jaguar is a very large cat that is
     feared by other animals.
It hunts other animals.

The jaguar lies flat on a branch.
It waits for an animal to walk by.
Along comes a peccary
     (PEHK-uh-ree).
It looks like a small pig.
The jaguar leaps down with a roar.
It lands hard on the peccary.

Lots of plants grow on the trees.
They are called air plants.
Their roots are in the air or on tree
limbs.

The bromeliad (broh-MEAL-ee-add)
is an air plant.
It grows on trees.
The plant looks like the top of a
giant pineapple.

The center of the bromeliad is like a
small pond.
It fills with rainwater.
Frogs, snails, and insects live in the
rainwater.

Few plants grow on the forest floor.
Too little sun comes through the
    canopy.

There are some large plants that do
    grow on the forest floor.
Rafflesia (raff-LEE-zuh) is one of
    these plants.
It has the world's biggest flowers.
Each flower is up to three feet
    across!

The forest floor is also home to
    many insects.

Many kinds of ants live here.
Some are army ants.
Army ants are very big.
They are brown or yellow.
Thousands of army ants sweep
    through the forest.
They look like troops on the march.
Army ants eat other insects most of
    the time.
But they also eat spiders or small
    animals.

Some rainforest animals eat ants.
One animal that eats ants is the
    collared anteater.
It has sharp claws to break open the
    ant nests.
And it has a long tongue to lick up
    the hurrying ants.

Rivers and streams run through the
    rainforest.
Many plants and animals live in or
    near the water.

A most amazing plant that lives in
    the water is the Queen Victoria
    water lily.
It has big round leaves.
Each leaf is up to six feet across.
A grownup could lie down on a leaf
    without sinking.

Giant anaconda snakes live near
the water.

They swim in the rivers of the
rainforest.

Anacondas eat birds and lizards.

They wrap themselves around the
animals.

Then they squeeze the birds and
lizards to death.

Lots of different kinds of animals
live in the water.

Some are like the manatees, or
sea cows.

These huge mammals can eat over
100 pounds of plants a day.

The piranha (pih-RAHN-uh) fish eats
seeds and nuts that fall into
the water.

Piranhas also eat small animals and
other fish.

Anaconda Snake

Manatee

Piranhas

People also live in the world's
     rainforests.
They live in homes on the forest
     floor.
And they live along streams and
     rivers.

One group of people who live in the
     rainforests of South America is
     the Yanomami (yah-no-MOM-ee).
Other tribes that live there are the
     Kayapo (ky-YAH-po) and the
     Boros.

SOUTH
AMERICA

Pygmies (PIG-meez) live in the
rainforests of Africa.

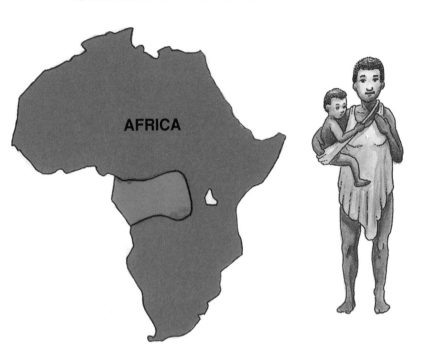

AFRICA

Penans live in the rainforests of
Malaysia.

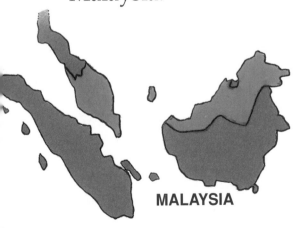

MALAYSIA

The Yanomami people stay in small
   villages.
Each village has a yano.
This is a big round house.
Everyone eats and sleeps in the yano.

The Yanomami women gather
plants and fruit.
They also grow crops outside the
village.
The men hunt animals.
Young Yanomami children play in
the village.
They also help their mothers.
As they grow older, boys and girls
do different things.

Boys hunt with their fathers.
The men form a line in the
    rainforest.
The boys go ahead without making
    a sound.

Then the boys run back to the men.
They shout and make noise.
This frightens deer, opossum, and
    other animals.
They come out of their hiding
    places.
The men shoot the animals with
    bows and arrows.
The animals are brought back to the
    village for food.

Girls and women work around the village.

They look for nuts and berries in the forest.

They gather firewood to cook the meals.

They harvest the crops.

Late in the day, the men and boys
come back from the hunt.
They cut up the dead animals.
The women toss pieces of meat into
big cooking pots.
Each family sits and eats around a fire.

Later, the families meet in the
middle of the yano.
The men tell the story of the hunt.
Someone starts to sing.
Others join in.
Soon everyone is singing and
dancing.

After a while, the people go to sleep.
Tomorrow is another day.
Everyone must hunt or work in the
   village.

Plants, animals, and people—
      they all live in the rainforest.
But many of them are in danger.
Do you know why?

Workers are clearing rainforest land
      —to raise cattle
      —to grow crops.

What happens next?

Rainforest people lose their homes.

Rainforest plants and animals lose their homes.

Then what happens?

Without rainforest trees the world
could change.

The air would be less healthy to
breathe because rainforest trees
provide most of the world's
oxygen.

The climate could grow warmer
without the protection of the
trees.

Some plants and animals that
can only live in the rainforest
would disappear forever.

We would not have some of the
important medicines that are
made from rainforest plants.

What can people in rainforest countries do?

They can stop cutting down the trees.

They can find other places to work.

They can use the rainforest without hurting it.

They can protect rainforest people, plants, and animals.

NATURE
PRESERVE

ANIMALS AND
PLANTS PROTECTED

DO NOT HARM
OR REMOVE

What can you do?

You can tell others about the rainforest.

You can join a group to save the rainforest.

You can raise money to save rainforest land.

You can stop buying things made of teak, mahogany, and other rainforest woods.

You can ask if a hamburger has been made from beef raised on rainforest land.

Rainforests are millions of years old.
They are among the oldest places
　　on earth.
They have more kinds of plants and
　　animals than any other place
　　on earth.
Let's keep them alive and well.

Index